In Sickness
and In Health

In Sickness and In Health

A STORY OF LOVE, STRENGTH, AND FAITH

Wesley Thompson

tandem light press

Tandem Light Press
950 Herrington Rd.
Suite C128
Lawrenceville, GA 30044

Tandem Light Press paperback edition May 2017

ISBN: 978-0-99767-8-6
Library of Congress Control Number: 2017936743

Biblical passages are from the King James Bible

Information in Chapter 9 on Anti-NMDA used with permission from antinmdafoundation.org

PRINTED IN THE UNITED STATES OF AMERICA

For my wife Tanndra and son Miles: because of you two I continue to fight through all adversities and not give up. For my family and friends: thank you for the outstanding support and prayers. Without them, I wouldn't be standing today.

Contents

Acknowledgments

I would like to thank all of my family, friends, classmates, ministry colleagues, and those who I'd never met before but took time to reach out to me with encouraging words. It's one thing to be told you're loved. It's another thing to be shown that you're loved. You all went far and beyond in showing my family how much you love us.

To various churches such as the New Calvary Missionary Baptist Church in Atlanta, Georgia, Providence Baptist Church in College Park, Georgia, Mount Calvary Missionary Baptist Church in Anniston, Alabama, First Baptist Church Of Stewardship in Atlanta, Georgia, Providence Missionary Baptist Church in Thomasville, Georgia, Galilee Missionary Baptist Church in Florence, Alabama, Elizabeth Baptist Church in Conyers, Georgia, Living Word Community Church in Florence, Alabama, Bethel Lauderdale Missionary Baptist Church in Florence, Alabama, and many others: thank you for giving us your prayers and giving to us out of your pockets to help us during such an unexpected time.

To the Stetson School of Business & Economics at Mercer University, McAfee School of Theology at Mercer University, and Mercer University as a whole: Thank you to all my co-workers, professors, and classmates for the phone calls, messages, and visits. I could not have chosen a better university to attend graduate school and work for than Mercer. You all will forever hold a special place in my heart. Go Bears! Also to Tanndra's employers, the Crossroads Hospice and Palliative Care in Tucker, Georgia and Fulton County Court Appointed Special Advocates (CASA) in Georgia. Thank you for your consistent sincere care and concern for our family during this period.

To the Emory University Hospital Midtown Neurological ICU staff and Maternity staff. The four months we spent at the hospital, you all became like family to us. The genuine concern and care you gave us was done out of your hearts and not just out of your duty. A four-month hospital stay is unthinkable to anybody. You all made it easier on us to get through.

To Pamela, Caroline, and the entire team at Tandem Light Press: thank you for making this writing, editing, and publishing process stress-free for me. Every time I had questions, you all were accessible and quick in answering them for me. I look forward to hopefully working with you all in the future!

Introduction

"It's important that we share our experiences with other
people. Your story will heal you and your story will heal
somebody else. When you tell your story, you free
yourself and give other people permission to
acknowledge their own story."
— Iyanla Vanzant

After twelve years of grade school, four years of
undergraduate school, three years of graduate school,
and currently almost a year into completing a doctorate
program, I've read a lot. In all my years of reading many
books from many authors, never did I think one day
someone would read a book written by yours truly.
Never did I think one day I'd have the title of "author"
placed in front of my name. If the thought did ever
come across my mind to write, I'm sure it would have
been a book about practical ministry, African American
Theology, or twenty-first century social justice, as those
are topics I have deep interest in. However, as you're
about to read through these upcoming chapters, this
book is about me. It's about my life. It's about my
experience. It's about my story. A story that's full of
misery, yet full of miracles at the same time. A story that
speaks about a storm in my life I never saw coming, yet

God blessed me in the midst of it as thunder rolled and lightening flashed. This is a story about a young husband, man, father, and pastor whose faith was tested in the most unusual unexpected ways. It's a story of love to one woman, faith in one God, and gift of one child. I hope for my story to bless and help four different audiences. Couples, men, fathers, and those in ministry.

One of my goals for this book is for it to bless those (particularly young people) who are either married or about to get married. It could perhaps be a source for marital enrichment and/or premarital counseling. I encourage you to mean what you say and say what you mean when you repeat "In sickness and in health" at the altar. It's difficult to stay true to that vow when you have fifty years of marriage under your belt and are both up in age. Imagine how difficult it is to stay true to it when neither of you have hit thirty yet. It was my true, real, and sincere unconditional love for my wife that kept me by her side during this story and still to this day. I never once thought about leaving her. Make sure your love for your spouse or soon to be spouse is at a similar level where you know if life took a sudden unexpected turn, you will stay grounded in the situation with him/her getting through it together.

Another goal for this book is for it to bless all my fellow men. Because of their natural ability and skills to nurture, the concept of caregiver is often associated with women. I've had to become a caregiver not only to my wife, but just as importantly to myself as well. As a man this experience has grown me in some areas I never knew existed, such as being open to share my feelings and not being ashamed to show my emotions. The experience of the story you're about to read ripped away what I thought masculinity to be, and showed me what masculinity really is. Masculinity entails crying, admitting when you're hurt, asking for help, being unashamed of struggles, and much more. Men, I want you to take away from this book that you cannot solely depend on your strength to get through everything that comes at you. It may have worked out so far for you now, but eventually something destructive will come along that's going to break you down. It's in those times you need to recognize the strength of God and the strength of genuine people to help you through.

My third goal for this book is for it to bless fathers. While I'm technically a soon-to-be father in the bulk of this story, I had to make some decisions to make sure fatherhood would still become reality for me. I functioned as, thought like, and acted like a father before *father* became an official title for me. My advice to those expecting their first child is to prepare yourself for fatherhood by doing and saying things as if you're a father right now. Don't wait. For those of you who have kids, simply love on them. If you and the mother of your child didn't go through any pregnancy issues, thank God. If your baby was full-term, thank God. If your baby had no complications after birth, thank God. If you got to take your baby home with you two or three days after birth, thank God. If you got to have a baby shower and take part in all the other festivities of being pregnant, thank God. It's so easy to take those things for granted. I never knew just how much pregnancy can change a woman's body to the point where something like our situation takes place. You'd be surprised at just how often it happens to people. Parenthood doesn't always start off easy for everyone for various uncontrollable reasons.

Lastly, a goal for this book is for it to bless those in ministry. In our roles as pastors/preachers, we're often mistaken for having it good in life. People view pastors as having it all together and problem free. Sometimes as pastors, we can mistakenly think that of ourselves. But when the faith we portray and preach on is tested, the question is who will encourage us? Who will preach to us? While you're covering your parishioners, as a pastor make sure you're covered as well. Make sure there's some people in your life who can speak a comforting word to you when your situation has dried up all of your sermonic abilities to the point where you can't even preach to yourself. Realize that your walk with God isn't always going to be down bright beautiful paths. There are going to be some walks in the wilderness. There are going to be some stops in a Gethsemane. It's in those moments you have to truly believe for yourself what you tell your parishioners to believe. That God is a healer. That God is a way maker. That God is a provider. That God is all we need God to be whenever we need God to be it.

I pray that each goal I've just outlined is accomplished for who it needs to be accomplished for. I pray my story opens your eyes to the fact that you too have a story. We all do. The question you must ask yourself is, "What am I doing with my story?" You'd be surprised just how much of an inspiration and blessing what you've gone through can be to somebody else. May you be inspired and blessed by what I had to go through and am still going through. I welcome you to my story.

1

J Do

"I found the one my heart loves,"
– Song of Solomon 3:4

May 18, 2013

The day was finally here. The moment that would solidify the other piece I needed to start my family dynasty. The moment where just as George, I would finally have my Weezy. Just as Heathcliff, I would finally have my Claire. Just as Uncle Phil, I would finally have my Vivian. Just as Martin, I would finally have my Gina. The moment that felt so far away as a child, but crept quickly upon me in the blink of an eye. The moment I would always tell friends it "would be some time," came abruptly. The moment that seemed surreal because of inattentiveness given to life's yearly calendar changing its four digits so rapidly. The moment that would change my entire life. The moment that would ensure me a permanent roommate, tag team partner, and sidekick.

Who would've thought this short, quiet girl—whose beauty I'd artfully found a way to glimpse without being noticed as I passed by the windowed office where she worked as a student worker—would be standing in front of me at this moment? Who would have thought the one who didn't give me a first date or first kiss at my request, but rather made me work hard to deserve both of them (the kiss came three months after the date if I may add), would be standing in front of me at this moment? Before I got that first date, Tanndra and I were in the courting stage. Many in the younger generations don't know anything about "courting" someone. That's an old-school term I heard my grandparents use when reminiscing back in their day. Courting is what you do before you start dating. It implies literally putting someone on trial in a courtroom. That is exactly how it felt when I began talking to Tanndra. She vetted and interrogated me to the max as a top-notch prosecutor would do an opposing witness. Nevertheless, the wait for the date, the wait for the kiss, the length of the vetting, and the intensity of the questioning was all worth it for this one moment.

She was the only person I wanted to share this moment with. To this day, friends considering taking their relationship to the next level often ask how I knew to ask Tanndra to marry me. How did I know she was the one? The answer wasn't as hard to give as I thought it'd be. I knew she was the one when I realized if something ever happened to cause us not to be together, I would not be able to find anyone else better for me. I wouldn't even want to attempt dating someone else. I chose her. I was all in. I knew whom I wanted, what I wanted from her, and where I wanted to take us together as a couple. Our minds connected. Our hearts connected. Our ambitions connected. Most of all, our spirits connected. When you have an untouchable confidence and assurance that she/he is the one and there's not an ounce of cynicism in the mix, it helps validate to you that you are ready to pop the question. This woman deserved to be more than just my girlfriend. She deserved to be my wife. She took me to court to get to know me before we began dating. Now I wanted to take her to court, in a literal sense, to give her my last name.

After four years of dating, I asked Tanndra to marry me on New Year's Day of 2012; that led us to this moment standing in front of a church full of family and friends to watch us exchange vows. We decided to stick with the traditional script that's recurred millions of times through wedding ceremony history.

As I held her hands and focused my eyes upon hers, the preacher asked me to repeat after him the age-old potent pledge. "I, Wesley, take you Tanndra to be my wedded wife. To have and to hold. To love and to cherish from this day forward. For better for worse, for richer or for poorer, in sickness and in health…"

I repeated each word with the utmost confidence. Every syllable rolled off my tongue and formed its enunciation from the pits of my heart. To me these vows were not just a contractual agreement made between man and wife. They were a covenantal assurance made between man and God. I didn't just take this pledge and promise to Tanndra serious at heart at the altar, I took it seriously at heart when I asked her to marry me.

If your promise of love, honesty, and commitment is just being solidified for the first time through a phrase you echo on your wedding day, then the union has already begun on a shaky foundation. The big question of "Will you marry me?" in actuality should be seen as a motion of vowed loyalty and love unto itself, while the wedding day ritual should serve as a second and all in favor of the motion. If your evolvement from engagement to marriage is viewed and executed in such a way, I guarantee it will strengthen the knot that will no doubt face its battles of attempted untying.

I undoubtedly affirmed this covenantal assurance I was making at the altar; however, I believed and hoped in nothing but blessings and prosperity for us. We loved and cared about each other too much for "worse" to ever have a chance at entering our relationship. We were both too fiscally smart and cautious for "poorer" to ever be an option in our household. You're reading the words of a person who goes directly to the clearance rack and wanders nowhere else every time I enter a department store. I am the one guy you see at Wal-Mart looking as if I'm making a life or death decision on whether I want to spend fifty cents more for trash bags with drawstrings or no drawstrings. Lastly, we were both too young and too healthy for "in sickness" to cast any of its ugly infirmities upon us any time in the immediate decades to come. I was twenty-four. She was twenty-six. Neither of us had ever received a negative doctor's report or been seriously ill. I was sure that time wouldn't come until late in our marriage, if at all; perhaps as retired grandparents in our seventies or eighties enjoying a cool spring breeze in our rocking chairs on the front porch.

I so looked forward to a long, happy, flourishing, and successful life with the woman I knew God created and molded just for me. Her beauty, intelligence, character, determination, and love of God reeled me in from day one. As we lit the unity candle, there was another candle set on a stand next to a picture of Tanndra's mother. Her mother passed away from brain cancer at the young age of thirty-six when Tanndra was only fourteen years old. Even though I never had the opportunity to meet her, I felt as though I had since Tanndra had spoken so much about her.

I vividly remember the moment we walked over to light that candle. Tanndra became very emotional with tears streaming down her face. This was the day every mother dreams of sharing with her daughter, and every daughter dreams of sharing with her mother. From shopping for wedding dresses, to picking floral arrangements, to contacting caterers, and to ultimately walking down the aisle, the process of getting to the wedding and culmination of completing the wedding day is certainly a concerted yet joyous tag team effort between bride and mother. It pained me knowing Tanndra was not able to experience that effort with her mother, along with so many other things in life. Conversations about boys, advice on dating, high school graduation, and help on choosing a college are things I'm sure many young women can take for granted having with their mom. Tanndra was not able to have any of it, yet she thrived to become an incredible woman that I know would've made her mother proud. I believe that's a reason her tears fell so much. Tanndra acknowledged to herself and to her mom, "Mom even though I hate you couldn't be here to see me succeed the way I have, know that the short fourteen years you had with me was enough to help me get to where I am."

I have never told Tanndra this, but I felt an overwhelming spirit come over me in that particular part of the ceremony. Tanndra had walked ahead of me to be closer to the picture to have personal time at that moment honoring her mother. Tanndra stood in between me and the picture of her mom. The spirit I felt was that of her mom telling me to be sure I take care of her daughter, love her daughter, do right by her daughter, protect her daughter, and to never leave her daughter by the wayside. It was a spirit telling me she did everything she could as long as God allowed her to raise and prepare an amazing gift. A gift now handed over to me to be accountable for and pour into my own unconditional love to increase her already rich value even more.

The call and challenge I felt from that spirit readied and excited me even further to culminate the ceremony with the two simplest yet powerful words one could ever say to their spouse. The preacher asked me the second most important question of my life (the first being do I accept Christ in life).

"Do you Wesley take Tanndra to be your wedded wife? To live together after God's ordinance in the Holy estate of marriage? Do you promise to love her, comfort her, honor her, and keep her in sickness and in health? And forsaking all others keep yourself only to her, as long as you both shall live?"

I proudly answered, "I do."

Saying "I do" on your wedding day shouldn't just be viewed as reciting a repeated phrase. It should be viewed as ratifying a revered promise. The things you're saying "I Do" to should matter to you just as much as it matters to the person you are saying it to.

I kissed her lips (which I've loved from day one, by the way) and we were on our way out. She walked down the aisle on her dad's arm, but now she walked back up the aisle on my arm. She walked down the aisle as Ms. Davis, but now she walked back up the aisle as Mrs. Thompson. She walked down the aisle with a veil covering her face, but now she walked back up the aisle with a husband covering her life.

After the ceremony, we took what seemed to be hundreds of pictures and were off to the reception. We walked into a warm welcome there, and I literally mean warm. The A/C in the building we used turned on when people arrived instead of turning on the morning of or night before, as it should have. That was not the best choice being it was a late May humid evening in Alabama with 200 plus people gathered. I have not met a couple yet whose wedding day went perfectly as planned. There is always at least one unexpected surprise. This happened to be ours. Nevertheless, we ate, danced, partied, and had lots of fun. Everyone enjoyed themselves. Tanndra and I ended the night in our hotel room eating delivery pizza from Domino's, and opening wedding gifts as if we were five-year-olds on Christmas morning.

The next morning, we flew out to Port Canaveral to hop on a cruise to the Bahamas for our honeymoon. I'd never been on a cruise before. I'd never traveled out the country before. Heck, I'd never traveled outside the South. There was no other person I would rather knock out all three than with Tanndra.

The fun we had was indescribable. While soaking in the sun together lying in chairs on Coco Cay beach, my mind wandered back to the rushing thrill of the past few days. This was the beginning of an everlasting God-favored journey of life and love. We were adamant on being together forever. Divorce would not be an option for our marriage. We had both come from families not whole due to divorce. My mom and dad were never married, and went on to both divorce individuals they did marry. Tanndra's mother and father were divorced, and went on to both divorce individuals they'd married again. Family history and statistics were definitely not on our side, but we declared to each other we would use our family dynamics as a motivator more than anything to make our marriage work no matter what. We were set on breaking the cycle. We had a tenacity to set a new standard. The vows I made to her meant something and I had a goal to fulfill them to the highest.

Looking back, it's ironic how the term "in sickness and in health" appeared twice in different segments of our ceremony script. I said "I do" to it, but little did I know it would eventually have significant impact and regard sooner than I'd thought.

2

On Top of the World

'Being on top of the world doesn't mean anything unless
you know what it's like to be at the bottom."
– Rachel Smith

May 2013 – July 2015

In the five years between us dating in college and
marrying, we made quite a few educational and career
moves. Tanndra graduated from the University of North
Alabama with a bachelor's degree for social work in 2009
and worked for a year before going back to school to
receive a master's degree in the same field from Alabama
A&M in 2011. From there she moved to Birmingham,
Alabama, for a social work job with the state. I'd
graduated from the University of North Alabama with a
bachelor's degree for political science in 2010, and
worked briefly with the federal government before
moving to Atlanta to attend Mercer University and
pursue a master's of divinity degree in 2011. When we
married in May 2013, I had one year left in the program.
Tanndra left her job in Birmingham to move to Atlanta
with me.

Our first year of marriage could not have been
better. We were a young couple both used to the rural
comforts of Alabama now living in the big city of
Atlanta. It took some time for us to get used to it, but to
our surprise we'd come to love the city lifestyle. At first,
we were gung-ho on moving back to our comfort zone

of security and familiarity in Alabama immediately after I finished school, but God had other plans. My ministry flourished in a way I had never imagined. In Alabama I had preached at churches with congregations of seventy to a hundred or so people. Now I was having opportunities to preach at churches with congregations of 3,000 people. I don't say that to downplay the smaller churches; I'm grateful and honored for every preaching opportunity I'm given no matter how many there are in front of me. I say it to convey that God saw fit to bless a young preacher from a backwoods country church like me to have a place and voice in some incredible settings I felt undeserving to be a part of.

Though the first year of marriage was great, it did not come without stressful times. Tanndra finding a job after moving to Atlanta became much harder than we anticipated. We both figured someone with her education, experience, and credentials would be hired on the spot. Little did we know it would take over a year. The only income we had came from my grad school student loan refunds and my twenty-hour-a-week 7.50/hour on-campus work-study job. The closer we got to my graduation the more nervous we became. Money was running out. There would be no more student loans or work-study checks. I didn't have job offers coming as I thought I would. When I graduated in May, we literally had just enough to cover expenses for the month of June. If things didn't work out, we knew moving back to Alabama with family would be our only option.

I had personally spent a lot of time praying alone about the situation, asking God to grant either of us (preferably both of us) a job to maintain self-sufficient living. Tanndra of course was praying the same thing in her personal prayers. It wasn't until we started praying together and lifting up our unified request to the Lord face to face and hand in hand that we started to see God move things in place for us. With no hope of having July's bills paid, Tanndra was hired the first week of June for a full-time supervisor position at a local non-profit organization that advocates for neglected children. I was hired the second week of June for a part-time position with the university I attended, and a month later it turned into a full-time position with the admissions department. I believe God's timing was intentional in this situation.

As the popular church song says, "He may not come when you want him, but he'll be there right on time. He's an on-time God yes He is." It matters to have a strong individual prayer life. All of us should have a personal prayer closet we enter into daily. It should be a closet where the floor is never dry due to the flow of tears coming from both a place of pain when we ask of God, and place of praise when God answers. It should be a closet where the walls are cracked and splintered from the loud outbursts of our voices conversing with God on every emotional level. It should be a closet in which the devil trembles at the thought of us entering because he knows everything he's trying to do against us will be overpowered by the one who is for us.

However, although it's an individual personal prayer closet, every so often it ought to have a special guest invited in if you're married. If your spouse has never been in your closet praying with you, then I urge you to make it happen ASAP! You will find things you've hoped for start coming to light when you're in the closet together. When you're in the closet together, arguments no longer become so big. Nerves will be rocked a little less; agreements start to take precedence over disagreements. When you're in the closet together, finances become a little easier to discuss. Family meetings will end on a good note. Planning for the future will start to create excitement instead of hesitancy. When you are in the closet together, the words "I love you," are actually felt more than they are heard. Troublesome things that happen may cause damage to your marriage, but will never destroy it. Most importantly, when you're in the closet together, it prepares the two of you to get through situations you never thought you had the endurance to handle until you've faced them.

God definitely answered the prayers we lifted up together to him in the closet. Things started looking up with both of us now having careers in Atlanta. Since we both had full-time incomes coming into the household instead of living off financial aid life-support, we put ourselves in position to work on big things for the future. We opened up a few savings accounts. We took Dave Ramsey's Financial Peace University classes to help us take steps toward becoming debt free. We started gravitating to a more enjoyable social life with friends. Tanndra eventually got a new job working in grief/bereavement, an area where she had always wanted to make an impact. I got a second job working part-time as an adjunct professor at another local university teaching religion classes twice a week. On top of that, I was in the final stages of being considered for the position of senior pastor at a church that I was excited about having the opportunity to possibly serve.

By this time, it was summer 2015. Life could not have been going any better for us. The prayers, faith, and hard work looked like they were finally paying off. Just when we thought things couldn't get any more exciting for us, Tanndra had some surprising news for me one evening. She informed me that she thought she might be pregnant. I was elated! Though we were not trying, we certainly did not hang our heads in shock or regret. Having children was something we'd always talked about, but never set a time frame on. She'd bought a pregnancy test for us to find out together and to our excitement, it was positive! Our household of two was on its way to become a household of three in just nine months. The reality of fatherhood never gave me a scare; it gave me a spark.

For so many years as a youth pastor I'd mentored kids, taught them values of life, instilled in them Christian faith, gave them advice when they dealt with issues at school or home, took them on trips to the mountains or the beach, and functioned as a sincere, honest role model many of them needed. I loved on them and many times poured into them when I myself barely had anything to give. I treasured being in such a position to do such things for so many young people, but now I looked forward to being in this position and doing these same things (plus more) for my own child.

One of the most memorable experiences I'll ever have in life is the first OB/GYN appointment we had. Not since our wedding had I felt a deeper connection with Tanndra. I felt a unique proudness come over me while sitting next to her holding her hand as she laid on the table being examined by the doctor. I often see social media statuses of people showing pictures of a loving family with the hashtag #Goals. That's what I felt in that examination room. The ancient ode "First comes love, then comes marriage, then comes [Tanndra] with a baby carriage," was now a reality in front of me. It was as if I'd completed the last level and/or goal of life's game. Love, then marriage, and finally family.

When the doctor showed us the live video imaging of what looked like a peanut moving around, I was in awe. Inside my wife was new life created by our love for and with one another. We then heard the loud thunderous roar of the baby's heartbeat and Tanndra began to cry. They were tears of bliss. She too knew this was us reaching our #Goals. The sweet little girl who lost her mom way too early but overcame such tragedy and developed into an outstanding woman of God, was now about to become a mom herself.

I knew she would be a great mother. In fact, that's one of the many reasons I married her. I didn't just marry her for the immediate things about her in front of me. I also married her for the imminent things about her that lay ahead for me. While dating, I saw a great girlfriend in front of me, but what propelled me to ask her to marry me was that I knew she would be a great wife later on ahead for me. While dating, I saw a woman who had a caring heart for all humankind in front of me, but what drove me to ask her to marry me was that I knew she could show that same caring heart as a great mother to my children later on ahead of me. While dating, I saw in front of me a woman of faith and of the church who was with me for who I was (simply Wesley) instead of for what I was (a pastor). What made me ask her hand in marriage was that I knew she only had intentions of being "my lady" instead of being a "First lady" later on ahead of me.

Don't make the important decision to shift your romantic relationship into marriage based on how you know your significant other to be now without giving thought to who or how he/she will be later. Now I know people can selfishly change (unfortunately sometimes for the worse) later in life, and it can be completely at no fault to the person they chose to marry. However, if you go into a marriage hoping that changes needed immediately will come inevitably, you are doing yourself no good. Marriage shouldn't be treated as a coin toss. It shouldn't be treated as a roulette table. Marriage should be entered into with complete confidence and trust in the future of the personality, character, and standards of the individual you're trading vows with.

I knew the greatness Tanndra possessed, and I also knew the greatness she still had ahead of her. I wanted to give myself to it, and I wanted to offer mine to her.

Together the greatness we held, while being guided by the God of ultimate greatness, could not be defeated.

We were on top of the world. Life could not have been any better. I was in the beginning stages of every successful man's dream: Young African American male who defied statistics by walking across a graduation stage (twice) instead of walking across a judge's courtroom. I was married to a beautiful, intelligent, accomplished woman who loved the Lord. Between the two of us there were four degrees in our household. We soon planned to make it six by beginning our doctorates. Our finances were stable and on the rise. We strategically laid out a savings plan. We were in the process of upgrading from an apartment to a house. All of our hard work and determination were paying off. We'd fulfilled the start of our God-commanded duty of being fruitful and multiplying.

Little did we know that in the midst of tremendous steps forward, a treacherous storm was brewing that had our names on it. Yes, we were on top of the world, but in the blink of an eye the world was soon on top of us.

3

J Don't Know

"What do you do when you don't know what to do?"

August 23 & 24, 2015

It was a normal Sunday. Tanndra and I headed to church early that morning, as was our routine. We were still on the high of our pregnancy, being just six days removed from our twelve-week appointment and ultrasound. We took a "Hamony Test" to find out the sex, but did not open the sealed envelope when it arrived in the mail. We planned to make that moment special by opening it together during a trip to Miami we were set to go on two weeks later for Labor Day weekend. I hoped for a boy, while Tanndra hoped for a girl. Only a handful of family and friends knew about the pregnancy so far. We planned to let everyone else know after our Miami trip.

On the way to church, we talked about our excitement of going to a show later that evening. We'd bought tickets to the Motown Broadway Musical that was in town. Tanndra mentioned she wasn't feeling well because she hadn't eaten. Her appetite had recently been all over the place. I called a friend and asked him to bring her something on his way since we'd already made it to the church.

As always, Tanndra and I went our separate ways once we arrived. I taught youth Sunday school while she was a part of the young women's small group Sunday school class. This particular Sunday I also directed the youth choir. The kids sounded amazing. We were halfway through service when my friend texted me saying he was too late to order breakfast. That's when I noticed Tanndra was not in her usual spot in the sanctuary. Our pastor signaled me over to tell me she was in a back room with one of the church nurses. I went to check on her to find she was feeling worse. She couldn't tell if it was because she hadn't eaten or not. I made a quick run to waffle house during the sermon and thankfully made it back right in time to direct the kids for the invitation song. Tanndra did not eat the food I'd gotten, which was unusual. She loves Waffle House and I'd brought her favorite breakfast meal.

Most often, we stick around after service chatting it up with members. This time as soon as our pastor gave the benediction we left and headed home. Tanndra still could not figure out why she felt bad. I thought she would feel better once we got home and took our ritual Sunday after church nap, waking up just in time to go to the Motown show. Strangely, Tanndra did not go to sleep. I napped alone. When I got up and started making moves to get dressed, I noticed she sat quietly on the couch. She still had not eaten anything all day. She looked tired and confused. I went to iron my clothes thinking she was only a few minutes away from joining me by getting ready, but she did not move. I asked if she was going to get dressed soon because it was almost time to go. She told me she couldn't go because of how sick she was feeling. This came to a surprise to me. She had talked all week about how much she looked forward to attending the show and we had already spent the money on the tickets. One thing neither of us do is waste money, so I knew whatever she felt had to be bad if she was willing to waste perfectly good tickets.

I was disappointed, but understood. I figured the pregnancy had her all messed up. I immediately made phone calls trying to give away the tickets to friend after friend, but it was such short notice no one could go. Tanndra stayed on the couch not saying too many words. I kept asking her if she wanted to eat, but she couldn't answer. I eventually went to pick up take out from a local soul food restaurant we liked, but she only ate a few bites. She still could not tell me what was wrong exactly, which piqued my interest. I suggested we go to the emergency room but she refused. Seeing as how she really didn't want to go, I didn't force the issue.

On into the night she could not sleep. She kept tossing and turning, which made me keep tossing and turning. About every thirty minutes she jumped sitting straight up from laying down. All of a sudden, about five in the morning, she began quivering very frantically. That was the moment I forced her to get up and dressed. We had not slept all night. I demanded to take her to the emergency room. She hesitantly got up saying she didn't need to go. With keys in hand, I was at the door waiting. She told me to sit down because she didn't want to waste a trip to the hospital. She said all she needed to do was eat and that would probably solve things. She ate a piece of toast, oatmeal, and orange juice, which was more than she had eaten collectively the day before.

By this time, we both had to be at work three hours later. I dreaded the thought of going in after being up for twenty-four straight hours. Tanndra assured me she felt better and we got dressed and went off to work. It was a normal Monday in the office for me. I had an inbox full of emails from people inquiring about degree programs over the weekend. It was going fine until I received a text from Tanndra around three p.m. She told me she wasn't feeling well at all and that she needed to go to the doctor. I immediately headed out the door to pick her up. Our jobs were only an eight-minute drive apart. When I pulled up one of her co-workers held her by the hand and gently guided her to the car. Tanndra had the same look of unease and confusion she had the day before on our couch. On the drive to the OB/GYN's office things felt mostly normal. She didn't talk much, partly due to being on the phone with the doctor's office to let them know we were on the way for a walk-in visit.

It wasn't until we got to the office and out of the car that I could tell something was off about Tanndra. It wasn't anything she said. It was the way she looked and carried herself as we walked from the parking garage to the office. When we sat down with the doctor things became very weird.

Anyone who knows Tanndra know that she is a detailed orientated person. She's always paid careful attention to her health and is the type of patient who may overwhelm a doctor with questions and excess information about how she's feeling. Which is why it shocked me when she had no words for the doctor when he asked simple questions. He kept asking her what was going on, but she kept giving the same response. "I don't know," she said. This also shocked the doctor, not because he was aware of how she usually interacts at appointments, but because he was getting "I don't know" to the simplest questions a five-year-old could answer if they felt sick.

Her demeanor became more withdrawn and melancholy, and was clearly recognizable by the doctor. He asked me if she had any history of anxiety or depression. I quickly said no. She's never had nor came anywhere close to having such diagnoses. The doctor said in his view it was clear she was in a "low emotional state," and assured us that it wasn't uncommon for women in the early stages of their first pregnancy. He suggested prescribing anti-depressants which Tan and I immediately declined. He then gave us a list of recommended psychiatrists for her to see as soon as possible. Although I scuffed at his anti-depressants proposal, I did take the list of psychiatrists. I was just as shocked as the doctor concerning Tanndra. Her confusion had me confused. On the ride home, the troubled feeling I'd had when we first arrived at the doctor's was increasing. Something just wasn't right, and I didn't know why.

When we got home, as the night progressed things became more weird and uncomfortable. Like the day before, Tanndra still had not eaten. Her look of confusion was turning into an all-around blank stare of nothingness. I noticed how she was beginning to mumble things to herself. At this point, there was no doubt that I was way past concerned. It seemed like she was having some kind of psychological imbalance going on. I couldn't wait for morning to come to call the list of recommended psychiatrists from the doctor. If possible, I'd planned to have her on someone's therapy couch as soon as day broke.

About ten o'clock that night, Tanndra burst out screaming, "Call 911! Call 911!" It startled me because the entire time before that she was just sitting with the blank stare mumbling to herself. Though startled, I did not jump to do what she requested immediately. I could see she obviously wasn't showing any signs of pain or discomfort. She was sitting on the couch the same way she had all night. I kept asking her what's wrong, but she continued screaming the same thing. "Call 911! Call 911!" I refused to do so. I could clearly see there was nothing wrong with her physically. When I declined, she became more erratic. This time yelling, "I'm dying! I'm dying!"

I did not want to cause her to go into an even bigger frenzy, so I called 911 and asked for paramedics. My suspicion that there was nothing physically wrong with Tanndra was still there, which I'm glad was true because it took the paramedics twenty minutes to arrive. Thank God she wasn't in need of any real emergency treatment. It would have been too late by time they got there.

Once they came in to see her, it felt just like the doctor visit from earlier. They asked basic questions and her response to all of them was "I don't know." They didn't know what to do. I'm sure they've never been called out on a run for what's supposed to be a medical emergency, and the person supposedly having the emergency is sitting calmly on a couch responding with "I don't know" to every question thrown at her. After checking vitals to see that everything was okay, they asked one more time if she needed to be transported to the hospital and we said no.

Once they left, my composure went out the door with them. I could not understand what was happening. Almost breaking down in tears, I bellowed at Tanndra to tell me what was wrong. I could no longer take the constant "I don't know" responses. I hoped for something to break through after my outburst, but what I got in return made me even more emotional.

Suddenly Tanndra started laughing. It was a very odd laugh. The best way to describe it is the laugh you'll hear from The Joker in a Batman movie. I took it very personally. Here I was clearly concerned with her well-being, doing everything I could to fix it, and she's laughing at it. In the snap of a finger, the laughing swiftly turned into crying. Then to laughing again. Then to crying again. She did this for about ten minutes, switching between the two every other minute. I could do nothing but stare clueless thinking to myself, "What in the hell is going on?" As Tanndra had responded so much throughout the day, the only response I could give myself as an answer was "I don't know."

We went on to go through yet another night of no sleep. Tanndra's speech and behavior continued to get stranger by the hour. I could not wait until eight a.m. so I could start calling the offices of the psychiatrists and psychologists on the OB/GYN's list. Clearly, Tanndra needed some help from a therapist. Call after call I was told either the doctor was not taking new patients at the time, or it would have to be a few days until I could bring her in to be seen. I thought to myself, "No wonder there are so many complaints and public outcry about it being so hard for people with mental issues to get help." It made me wonder how many times there have been individuals with more severe need than Tanndra whose condition never recovered because it took too long for them to be seen.

I was stuck. Echoing hers, my answer now became "I don't know" to everything. I didn't know what was in my wife's mind. I didn't know why or how she'd gone from being herself to being someone I'd never seen before. I didn't know if I needed to take her to a mental facility or to the emergency room. I didn't know whom to call anymore. I didn't know if I should wait it out another day or take quick action. I didn't know what the outcome of all this would be. What I did know is that I was scared. I was puzzled. I was nervous. And I was praying.

4

Is This Really Happening?

"The world is so unpredictable. Things happen suddenly, unexpectedly. We want to feel we are in control of our own existence. In some ways we are, in some ways we're not..."
–Paul Auster

August 25, 2015

Things became worse as the morning waned on. It could not have come at a poorer time. The school where I taught as an adjunct started a new session of classes that night and I was scheduled to teach a class with fourteen students. I'd never had to cancel class before. It pained me to do so, but I needed to take care of Tanndra and I knew it wouldn't be solved in a few hours when it was time for me to leave.

It was obvious that Tanndra was present physically, but not cognitively. Never had I encountered interaction with my wife like this. She was not herself. She was in another dimension. I can still see the look on her face. It was as if she was having an out of body experience. She was in another world. Her face was fixated toward mine, but she was looking past me instead at me. She was having a conversation, but it wasn't with me. She was engulfed in talk with whomever or whatever it was giving her company in the strange place she was in. She began talking to herself even more, saying the same things repeatedly. I tried my best to engage with her, hoping I could gain access to what felt like coded language, but she responded with nothing different.

She kept repeating the same phrases. "Did that just happen?" "I don't know." "No." "Stop it." "Wesley save me." "God's got it." "We're going to be alright." "I'm going to be alright." I responded to each phrase with a question such as "Did what just happen?" "You don't know what?" "What do you need me to save you from?" I never got an answer. The only words coming out of her mouth were these phrases.

The phrase I vividly remember her echoing the most was "Is this really happening?" This was the only phrase she repeated consecutively without the others in between. She went back in forth saying it in a whisper, and other times in a loud voice. It was apparent she wasn't asking me this question directly. Neither was she asking it of herself. I could sense she asked this to someone, but it was someone only she could see. Only someone she could hear. Only someone she could feel.

I continued calling therapists and psychiatrists in the area, but still no luck. I decided to call a mental crisis hotline. After answering what seemed to be hundreds of questions, the representative informed me she would have a crisis team come over to observe and assess Tanndra. Before they arrived, Tanndra's bizarre speech trickled over into more bizarre behavior. She got dressed as if she were going to work, grabbed her purse, keys, and walked out the door. I stopped her before she proceeded to walk down the stairs of our second-floor apartment. I asked her what she was doing and where was she going. She didn't answer. In fact, it was as if she didn't even hear or see me. She turned around, walked past me, and went back inside only to do the same thing. She took off the clothes she had on and got dressed again in something different, grabbed her purse, keys, and walked out the door. I let her walk down the stairs this time. She looked confused once she got to the parking lot. Her car was still at her job from when I picked her up the day before. After informing her of that, she turned around walking past me without a word to go back inside only to do the same thing again. She changed clothes and walked outside five different times. I finally stopped her from going back out by blocking the door. She then went back to repeating, "Is this really happening?"

By this time, I was as confused, surprised, and at a loss more than I'd ever been. When the two-woman crisis team arrived, I filled them in on everything that had transpired to this point. One of the women was around our age, and the other maybe in her fifties. They tried to speak with Tanndra, but she wouldn't give a normal response. She sporadically repeated the phrases she'd been saying throughout the day. She then began to cry out of nowhere. This time it wasn't blended with laughs like the night before. It was obvious these were tears coming from a troubled person. When asked why she was crying, Tanndra only shook her head continuing to let the tears flow. The crisis team pulled me to the side to speak privately and said without hesitation, "Your wife is having a mental breakdown and you need to get her to a hospital as soon as possible." I asked what made them think it was a mental breakdown. They said from their professional assessment and observation, all the signs Tanndra gave off signaled it. They gave me some instructions on following up with them once we reached the hospital.

When I helped Tanndra gather things to leave, there was a difference in her. I no longer saw an oddness about her; rather I saw fear. She looked afraid. Perhaps she was coming back to herself a little and realizing something wasn't right. I took her to the hospital we went to for OB/GYN visits as it was the closest to where we lived. I was also personally familiar with this hospital; I interned as a chaplain there during my CPE (Clinical Pastoral Education) while in seminary.

When we arrived at the ER to check in, it was hard to explain the reason we were there. I pretty much repeated the report the crisis team had given me an hour earlier. During the wait to be called to the back, Tanndra began to speak more sensibly than she had in two days. She was able to tell me the passcode to her cellphone so that I could retrieve some important information. She was able to fill out some of the medical history form. She even asked a few questions about why we were at the ER. Apparently, she couldn't recall the fiasco that led us there. I could still see fear and even shock all over her face. However, I was relieved to at least be able to have somewhat of a clear conversation with her.

The ER receptionist finally called us to the back. I gave a rundown of what was happening to the nurse. I took initiative to answer all medical questions because I figured Tanndra might go back into her "I don't know" responses if asked. The nurse took some vitals that turned out to show not so good reports. Both Tanndra's blood pressure and heart rate were higher than normal. They could not find a reason for it. They did an ultrasound on the baby to make sure things were okay and thankfully they were.

Then all of a sudden, the unimaginable began. Utter chaos erupted in the small room we sat in, and found its way through the hallways of the entire ER like a tornado picking up more strength as it destroys everything in its path. What was the chaos? It was simply and solely Tanndra.

There was an abrupt personality change in Tanndra as she laid on the ER gurney waiting for the nurses to come back for another report. She moved her body awkwardly as if she was trying to get out of her own skin. I tried to ask her what's wrong and if everything was okay. She responded by reverting to the repeated phrases of earlier. "No. Stop it. I'm gonna be alright. What just happened? Is this really happening?"

Only this time she's saying it loudly in anger. In fact, she was yelling it to the point where people walking by the room stopped to look to see what was going on. The nurses tried to help me calm her, but she was becoming more riled by the minute. She started to forcefully pull back and kick as we were trying to physically keep her body calm and steady. She was still hooked up to the heart rate and blood pressure monitor. They both continued to increase along with her rough behavior. The nurses called in for more help and decided to inject her with something to calm her.

I felt tricked. Just when she was coming back to herself by being somewhat lucid and aware of her current state, not only did she backtrack but she warped into a zone I couldn't even explain. A doctor came in to tell me they wanted to do an MRI scan to check things. The nurses made me come along just in case she cranked up again, which was a good call because she did as soon as we got to the scan room. They gave her another injection that put her to sleep. When the MRI finished, they rolled her back to the ER room where soon after the dosage seemingly wore off and she became frenzied again. This time the physical behavior worsened to where she kicked at the nurses attempting to reconnect the leads attached to her chest.

As much as I tried to soothe her, it didn't work. She was a different person. Never before had she portrayed this character and conduct. The doctor came back into the room to let me know the MRI scan showed nothing. He too seemed a little puzzled. He called upon other doctors to observe Tanndra and to review her chart. After group contemplation, they concluded that she might have contracted viral meningitis, which is known to cause changes in thought and behavior. In order to test for it I had to sign approval for them to perform a spinal tap. I asked as many questions as I could think of to make sure the procedure would be safe during the pregnancy, and gave them the okay to do so after being assured of it. Because the spinal tap requires inserting a needle into the spine and is precisely sensitive, they injected Tanndra again to make her numb and put her in a temporary sleep.

When they finished, the entire medical staff cleared the room leaving me alone there with a sleeping Tanndra. By now, we'd been at the hospital nearly five hours. I took the quiet, lonely time to make phone calls to a few family members letting them know all that had gone on the past forty-eight hours, and that we were currently in the ER. As I tried to explain, I was reminding myself just how odd everything was. It was hard for me to verbalize it because this wasn't a flu, or an allergic reaction, or a pain in the abdomen. This was downright indescribable. Everyone I spoke with had the phone in one hand and their keys in the other hand headed out the door, but I asked them to stay put. I didn't want them getting on the road so late and driving for hours because I was hopeful we'd get some answers, be treated, grab some meds, and be on our way back home in just a few hours. However, I would soon find out that optimism proved to be so far from reality.

By the time I wrapped up the last phone conversation, Tanndra began to wake up. Her speech was slurred as she mumbled a few words I couldn't make out. I'd hoped the murmuring was due to being drugged up by the injections and not a continuation of what got us there in the first place. Unfortunately, to my disappointment, it was the latter. As her voice grew louder, I was able to make out the words. She was repeating what I'd heard all day long. "Is this really happening? No, stop. Wesley save me. What just happened? Is this really happening?"

With the increase in her volume also came the increase in her behavior. She began to strip off the monitor leads and tried to pull out her IV. The nurses came back into the room to help me contain her from causing harm to herself by taking needles out of her arm. They gave her another injection that quickly put her into another soft sleep.

I was getting very frustrated by this point. Frustrated from being hungry. Frustrated from being tired (neither of us had slept in the past forty-eight hours) and we'd been in the hospital seven hours. Frustrated from seeing my wife shot up with all these injections because whatever this was taking over her body was making her a wild, combative person.

The doctor came back to inform me that the spinal tap test results wouldn't be ready until the next day, so they were going to admit Tanndra into the ICU for the night. I questioned that decision. I asked him, "Why the ICU? Is it that serious?" He replied telling me that because there was a possibility of viral meningitis, it was in her best interest health wise and typical medical protocol to have her in ICU instead of out on the general floor.

It was definitely not the news I wanted to hear. I hadn't brought a change of clothes, a phone charger, or eaten because when we left home I assumed we would be back home the same night. I never expected she'd be admitted to stay in the hospital overnight, let alone on the ICU floor. The transfer process from the ER unit to the ICU upstairs took hours. It was two a.m. when we finally switched rooms. Tanndra was still asleep from the sedative on the way up, but on arrival began to wake again. This time it wasn't as subtle as the last. She threw what was no doubt one of the most extreme deranged fits the nurses ever saw. I'm not sure if it was because she woke up in a new room or because she woke up to see needles/wires attached to her body, but it seemed as if she never knew she was in the hospital and awoke in a reaction of fear. She ripped the IV out of her arm so forcefully that blood gushed down her arm. She pulled away the monitor leads and was on her way out of the bed before I got there to stop her.

The nurse rushed in to help me, but we could not keep her still enough to reinsert everything. As she fought us I noticed how strong she'd become. With her petite stature, Tanndra has never been the type to lift weights religiously, however she seemed to have obtained a supernatural strength out of nowhere. The nurse and I were quickly joined by six others (including security) surrounding her bed, all of us holding her down, so the IV could be placed back in her arm. Once it was in, they injected her with the same sedative that had calmed her earlier, but it didn't work this time. She kicked and punched at everyone around the bed including me. She did not want to be there. She was looking at the door wanting to get out of the room.

As the power of eight people holding her finally started to tire her, the nurses used restraints to tie her hands, arms, and legs to the bed. Tanndra never liked the feeling of being trapped. She would always get mad when I purposely yet playfully squeezed her body tight preventing her from moving. She hates feeling physically confined. Therefore, when the restraints were on she became furious.

Suddenly Tanndra looked up at me. Not past me or beyond me, but she looked at me. As she looked she yelled, "Wesley stop it! Why are you doing this? Why are you helping them? I just want to go. I don't want to be here. Why are y'all doing this? Stop it Wesley!" It was the first time in the past two days I sensed that it was her looking at and talking to me. It wasn't some other personality controlling her. The person looking at and speaking to me was the person I knew to be my wife, but unfortunately the position she was looking at me from and the words she spoke to me were not what I wished to see or hear. Her yelling transitioned into weeping as tears flowed down her face. Her anger turned into fear. It was as if she woke up and finally came to herself after being out of mind for over forty-eight hours. She could not understand why I was amongst these unknown people forcing her body into bondage to the hospital bed. She was scared and calling out to me for help, but I couldn't be the help she needed because I was a part of the very thing that was haunting her.

It tore me up inside. I will never forget the way she looked at me. For the first time in her life, Tanndra was scared of me. Never had I emotionally or physically abused her. Never had I verbally assaulted her. Never had I domestically neglected her. Since we'd been together, I gave her nothing but love, commitment, and security. Now for the very first time (from her point of view), I was an enemy to her. I'd caused harm to her. She was afraid of me.

Astonishingly something else happened for the first time also. For the first time in seventeen years, I cried. I felt the soft drops of wetness in between the small spaces of my nose and cheeks. I felt the salty taste of tears as they found their way down to my lips. The wall of vulnerability I'd done so well to uphold for so long to keep from crying, had been infiltrated.

Until this moment, the last time I'd cried was when my six-year-old brother tragically and unexpectedly passed away. I was ten years old. Since then I have had instances come about where I felt tears circulate on the inside, but they never made their way to the outside. When the nurses and security saw I was getting emotional, they escorted me out of the room as they continued to settle Tanndra down. I found my way to the end of the hallway near an elevator. It was a small, quiet place. With Tanndra's frightful sight and sounds still fresh, I bent down and just let everything I felt all out.

One would think since this was my first time crying in nearly twenty years that it would just have been a minor sob. It was the exact opposite. In fact, I believe nearly twenty years' worth of imprisoned tears decided to make a rush out of the wells of my eyes all at once during this rare moment of freedom I allowed. I was in another zone. I couldn't believe what had taken place up to this point. Not only could I not help my wife, but she clearly just saw me as an antagonist to her demise. As a husband, there is no worse feeling to have than the one I felt. Tanndra pleaded for me to help her. She begged me to save her. Yet from her point of view, I contributed to the very act she needed help and saving from. The way she looked at me was heart breaking. It was as if I'd left her alone to a pack of wolves and walked away.

Realizing the impossible had just taken place, I quickly tried to gather myself together. I literally punched myself in the chest as a sign to "man up" and turn off the water works. Now that I look back on it, that moment of weeping was actually one of the manliest things I've done in life. I gave in to vulnerability at a time when anyone would and should have expected me to do so.

When I stood back up, I literally stood in a pool of tears. One of the security guards came over and placed his hand on my shoulder telling me things were going to be okay. Right before I walked back into the room they'd given her yet another sedative that finally put her out. She was sound asleep. The nurse looked like she just finished working an emergency mass disaster. She was clearly tired and ruffled. That how's explosive Tanndra's behavior had been all night. She informed me that in all of her years of nursing, she'd never seen or heard of one person getting that many injections before being out. She said usually the first dose would knock out a 250-pound man, which made it hard to believe Tanndra's 5'0 frame required so much.

I asked her how long she thought we would have to be there. She said everything relied on the spinal tap results and until those came back, we were staying put. She left the room and I found my way to a seat. It was the first time I'd sat down since being in the waiting room ten hours earlier. I was still somewhat in the zone I found myself in a short time ago at the end of the hallway, only this time without the tears. As I watched Tanndra sleep, I understood how she felt. All day while in her uncanny state of mind she'd repeated, "Is this really happening?" Now that she was sleep and I still stayed awake, her words trickled into my consciousness. The only thing I could say to myself as I was alone. "Is this really happening? Is this really happening? Is this really happening?"

5

Tears

"Heaven knows we need never be ashamed of our tears,
for they are rain upon the blinding dust of earth,
overlying our hard hearts. I was better after I had cried,
than before."
— Charles Dickens

August 26-28, 2015

I didn't get much sleep staying overnight in the ICU room. I was somewhat jealous of Tanndra because her hospital bed looked a whole lot more comfortable than the contraption they called a reclining chair I laid on. When morning came, she was still asleep. I still had on the same clothes from the morning before and hadn't bathed or brushed my teeth since then. I took a quick trip home to shower and grab some things to take back to the hospital. I made calls to other family members I hadn't spoken with yet to let them know what was going on. A few were on their way from various states to check on her.

Once I made it back to the hospital, I had multiple conversations with the medical team caring for Tanndra. The doctor I had the most contact with was the Infectious Disease Specialist. He informed me the results of the spinal tap would likely take a day or two because the lab was backed up. From the report he received, he was leaning toward a diagnosis of viral meningitis. He'd asked me if we'd been out the country or made any camping trips recently, as these are the most likely ways to contract the disease. I chuckled before answering because Tanndra is afraid to go out of the country. She doesn't like the thought of flying over the ocean. In addition, she is not an outdoor person so camping is far from being one of her recreational activities. I wasn't sure of the severity of such a diagnosis, but at that moment I just wanted answers. Nothing made sense to anyone, including the nurses and doctors.

When Tanndra awoke, the only logical awareness she had was knowing me. She would call my name, but still in a way that seemed like she was in another world mentally. She kept having spurts of physical agitation where she'd try to pull out her IV and get out the bed to walk out of the room. The nurses had no choice but to keep the restraint straps on her arms, hands, and ankles. I would take them off whenever I was in the room keeping a close eye on her, but there were times where even I had to force her to keep them on because she was noncompliant.

The next day the test for viral meningitis came back negative. The Infectious Disease Specialist who was very perplexed by the results suggested a redo of the test. Because Tanndra's behavior and mental state seemed to slowly be growing more fitful, his experience and medical gut instinct insisted it had to be the meningitis. I'd never encountered anyone with that particular ailment so I wasn't sure what to look for. Something inside told me this was much more complicated though—there were too many random symptoms for it to be something they could quickly put a name to. The mental lapses she showed had taken me aback. I conferred with a friend who has a medical background for help. I was starting to become impatient with the hospital's lack of answers and the time it was taking to get back test results.

Another two days passed and Tanndra's vitals continued to fluctuate all over the place. I still could not get a coherent conversation out of her. She was trapped in what I can only describe as a mentally ill-like state of mind. The second viral meningitis test results came back as negative again. By this time, the doctors were kind of in a stalemate hoping that Tanndra would show signs of improvement on her own eventually. Perhaps it was some type of virus that couldn't be detected and just needed time to work its way out her system. This is what they told me and I accepted it. I thought it could be true when out of the blue on an early afternoon Tanndra seemed to snap out her irrational mindset. After being asleep most of the morning she opened her eyelids and turned to me. I was the only person in the room. I immediately noticed there was no agitation coming from her. She didn't become distressed or attempt to jump out of the bed, racing toward the exit as if she was an Olympic hurdler and runner. Instead, this time she was subtle and seemed unsure of where she was. It was as if she'd woken up and had no idea what took place over the last few days.

I hurriedly stood over her, softly swiping my hand across her forehead as I'd always done whenever she rested so beautifully peaceful. Pointing to the cords connected to her and machines buzzing she asked, "Wesley what is this? Is this the hospital? Why am I here?" She looked at me with much interest as I broke down this lengthy strange story of events that occurred in which she was the key player and actor, but she could not recall one scene of it. As I kept expounding, she wanted more details. That's how I knew this was Tanndra all the way. Anyone who knows her is aware that she is a person who wants all the facts about every little thing. Especially when it comes to her health. That's why she asked the nurse to come in to repeat everything I'd just stated. She needed expert confirmation.

She took in all the information we threw at her pretty well. The nurse was surprised at the sudden 180 degree change she seemed to have made overnight. Tanndra asked if she could have some water and as the nurse walked out to get it, she gave me a grin behind Tanndra's back as to say, "I told you she'd get better soon." This same nurse was there from the first day and saw the worry I'd gone through the whole week. Tanndra and I continued to talk about various things concerning how she got to the hospital. We even spoke about continuing our plans to go to Miami for Labor Day weekend. About an hour and half passed by since she'd woken up and I was able to enjoy speaking with the person who I knew as my wife instead of some demented alter ego. I appreciated our time alone together. The nurse was kind enough not to intrude too much and kept the door shut. She herself was anxious to inform the doctors about the quick change. Unfortunately, she didn't get the chance to.

After she was as normal, clear, and coherent as she'd ever been all week, suddenly in the middle of our conversing Tanndra harshly became stiff. Her eyes, no longer fixated on me, slowly began to roll to the back of her head as her body began to jerk violently. As she sat on the edge of the bed, I could see her begin to fall back. I wrapped my arm around her gently laying her on the bed so that she wouldn't hit her head too hard as the jerking became more forceful. I yelled for the nurse. She along with others came rushing in. For the first time in her life, Tanndra was having a seizure. Just before I could get out the way to turn her over to them, Tanndra started to foam at the mouth. It rapidly guzzled through her lips, which caused her to choke profusely.

That's when I lost it…

At that moment, my mind traveled back two years earlier when I did my chaplain internship for seminary at the same hospital. Hospital chaplaincy is a tough emotional job. Everyday you're called upon to enter private personal family situations in instances when death has just ravaged their lives. Chaplains face a range of duties such as being asked hard questions about death, thinking of the right words when a family asks for prayer, and even sometimes being the person to call a funeral home for the family to retrieve their loved one's remains. During my training my CPE supervisor expressed how I would eventually find out the hard way the fact that no matter how much training received, nothing really prepares you for the first death call you receive. I found out just how true that was.

I was the only chaplain on-call overnight. I received a "code blue" call on my beeper that came from the ICU floor. When I arrived doctors, nurses, and technicians filled the room out into the hallways. It was obvious this man's current state was grim. After much time spent working to revive him, the medical team unfortunately could not succeed. He'd died from asphyxiation during his sleep. When I walked in the room the stench from the vomit he'd choked on was fresh in the air. I could see it all over his mouth down to his chest. I learned even more came up through his esophagus as the medical team worked on him, which made it tougher for them to bring him back. An eerie feeling came over me. I stood in front of someone who'd just transitioned from life to death just two minutes ago. Just as any other hospital or hospice chaplain will tell you, we never forget having to go to our first death visit. It's a memory that vividly sticks with you. The room this man died in just happened to be down the hallway from Tanndra's room when her seizures occurred.

That's why I lost it. As I saw vomit gulp through her mouth in between the frenzied coughs, I remembered what had happened just down the hallway with the eighty-seven-year-old gentleman two years ago. I immediately thought the worst of the worst. As more people flooded the room to see about her I had Deja Vu all over again, but this time it was my wife who was going to die from asphyxiation.

I had one of those moments where you're so overwhelmed with emotion that you seem to have no control of your movement or your speech. The only thing I remember is running out of the room screaming and crying as I yelled to people around me, "This is not good! I've seen this before!" I kept repeating it as I looked in the room from the outside. I couldn't see Tanndra because there were so many medical staff bursting through the door. I honestly did not want to see her. I couldn't fathom watching my wife die.

My commotion and unrest was obvious to the staff around me. I was shaking, crying, yelling, and most of all fearful. I overheard one of the nurses tell another to call a chaplain to come up to be with me. That's when I realized I'd stepped foot into another dimension never visited before. For the first time in my life I wasn't the calm, cool, and collected person I'm known for being. For the first time in my life, I couldn't keep my emotions together. For the first time, people got a free open screening of my pain and fear. I was unable to raise my shield of privacy as was my custom. For the first time in my life, I needed a chaplain instead of being called in as a chaplain. For the first time, it was my heart that needed consoling instead of me consoling another's. For the first time, it was my tears seen and cries heard that prompted immediate help instead of me going in to help someone else.

I realized this the moment I overheard the nurse calling in a chaplain for me, and I immediately checked myself. I literally slapped my face and told myself to get it together. I was angry with myself for unravelling in front of people the way I did. I couldn't believe I'd lost it like that and I quickly wanted to gather my composure before anyone else saw me.

* * *

As I harken back on that moment, I now get angry with myself for getting angry with myself. In a time of pure fear and utter disarray, I did not allow myself to properly respond to what I saw and felt. Instead, I forcefully cutoff the outlet available to release my hurt and pain. A mistake I've made far too often before this moment, and something I believe we as men have issue with.

Many of us feel obligated to take on a superman persona when it comes to our feelings and emotions. We tuck away tears, words, anger, concerns, and grief into a place so far deep that we intentionally want them to be unreachable. Doing this benefits us absolutely nothing. If anything, it's an act of selfishness. We're being selfish to ourselves and to those who care about us most.

If we are to look at how a man should appropriately express himself in times of hardship, then I don't think there's a better example than that of David of the Bible. Through the Psalms alone, David admits his faults, pleas for forgiveness, cries, voices his depression, speaks anger, and seeks isolation. To say David wore his emotions on his sleeve would be an understatement. Yet he was okay with carrying those emotions all while still being a king, a warrior, a protector of people, and that beloved Biblical figure which we often refer to as being the "man after God's own heart." In other words, David represented ultimate "manliness" while at the same time embracing his personal sensitivity. I would like to make the claim that we shouldn't ever separate the two. Manliness *is* carrying your emotions. Manliness *is* embracing your own sensitivity. As men, if we are able to view our manhood in this light, we can make it easier on ourselves when tough stretches come about.

* * *

From the moment her seizure began, I was actually on the phone with Tanndra's father. She'd just briefly said hi to him. I was giving him an update telling him how well she seemed to be doing until the seizure happened. I realized I still had the phone to my ear amidst all the yelling and hollering I did. I scared him to death. As I became calmer, I also calmed him letting him know the medical team was slowly leaving the room one by one. They assured me she was okay and whatever they'd done to stop the seizure put her to sleep. Still shaking in my shoes, I peeked in to check on her wondering how things would be when she awoke.

I then walked back to the spot I found myself at the first night. The small corner at the end of the hallway near the staff elevator. As I'd done that night, I again dropped down to the floor and wept. However, there was something different about these tears. I felt a physical relief as they fell. As they flowed out, so did the fear and nervousness that'd just overtaken me moments ago. This time no one came to check on me, which was a good thing. I needed that time alone. I needed that time to let the adverse mood I felt come out of me through my crying.

Therapist Dr. April Wells once said to me, "Tears have language. What does yours say?" On that day, my tears spoke anguish, distress, panic, and uncertainty. I could relate to a mighty yet emotional King David when he said, "I am worn out from my groaning. All night long I flood my bed with weeping and drench my couch with tears." (Psalm 6:6)

6

Stuck Between a Seizure and a Steeple

"Fear and faith have something in common. They both
ask us to believe in something we cannot see."
— Joel Olsteen

August 28-30, 2015

Later that day when Tanndra awoke, we were back at
square one. She was very disoriented and incoherent in
both her speech and thinking. The progress I'd noticed
just hours earlier was lost in such a quick moment's time.
Her surprising seizure threw the doctors for even more
of a loop in trying to figure out what on earth to name
this.

Family members began arriving to Atlanta to see about
her. Her father, sisters, brother, aunts, uncle, cousin, best
friend, and my mother all traveled from various states. I
was so relieved to have them present. For the first time in
days, I was finally able to get some rest in my own home in
my own bed. Even though I explained the best way I could
the situation to everyone over the phone, they were still
shocked to see for themselves what was going on. Tanndra
is one of the most intelligent, competent people you'll
meet, so to see and hear her so mentally unstable
stunned the family. They've known her longer than I

have so you could only imagine how much it hurt them knowing this was not the Tanndra they knew at all.

Tanndra and I both are very private. Therefore, the only people who knew what happened thus far were a few family members. The more I realized she wasn't going to snap out of this quickly and the doctors struggled to figure out answers, I decided to confide in a few special friends I could trust. I sent out a mass text message to about twenty close friends letting them know about the situation and petitioned their prayers. These were people I knew had a strong prayer life and dedicated relationship with Christ. I couldn't just ask anybody to pray for her at this time. I needed some prayer warriors whose supplications God would no doubt receive and hear.

Everyone responded with grave concern and promised to lift us in prayer. One of these close friends was the pastor of a church in the area and asked me if I'd come preach the coming Sunday if I was up for it. He knew, as most preachers would agree, that standing before the people behind the pulpit delivering a word from the Lord is just as comforting to the speaker as it is the hearers. My pastor in Atlanta, Reverend Pozie Redmond, once told me that there are many times on Sunday mornings he wakes up and doesn't feel like preaching whether it's due to sickness, stress, or physical fatigue, but he finds the will to get to the church anyhow. Even though he still feels the same way up to the point of service starting, once he walks out of his office and turns the corner to enter the sanctuary something comes over him. He described it as a rush of energy and new excitement knowing he's getting ready to partake in the preaching moment. All the sickness, stress, and tiredness goes away right before he walks through the doors and he stands boldly in the pulpit proclaiming God's word with authority.

That's the power of preaching for the preacher. We go in knowing we have the responsibility to help the people, but also knowing what takes place will help us also. For those who cannot understand, just know that in our times of distress the act of preaching is a form of therapy for the preacher. When we belch out "God will make a way out of no way," we're not just talking to you, but we're talking to ourselves as well. When we scream, "God is able," we're not just talking to you, but to ourselves as well. When we shout, "The Lord will bring you out," we're not just talking to you, but to ourselves as well. Preaching is therapeutic to the preacher because when we pray asking God to allow the preached word to heal broken hearts, in many occasions it's our own hearts that's broken the most out of anyone in the room. Yet we trust in and lean on the almighty God who gave us this sacred calling which enables us to preach through our pain.

I graciously accepted my friend's invitation to preach at his church that Sunday. In the meantime, Tanndra gained a little progress in her ability to recognize her family and speak to them on a clear level. They all stayed for two days before returning home, but assured me they would be back the next weekend if she was still hospitalized. Her youngest sister Donya stayed here to help give me breaks throughout the days and nights by staying at the hospital with Tanndra. Donya graduated with her bachelor's degree just three months prior and had recently moved to Virginia with one of their aunts in hopes of finding a job or possibly starting graduate school. Therefore, she was in a place where she could sacrifice the time to stay which proved to be such a lifesaver down the road.

Tanndra's heart rate and blood pressure still fluctuated all over the place. Whenever it jumped sky high, the doctors/nurses injected a medicine called

Ativan into her IV to bring it down. Her heart rate stayed at around 150 and the lowest the medical team could get it without giving her too much of the medicine was about 120. Other than that, progress seemed to continue. In fact, one of the doctors mentioned if they could get her vitals to stay at a normalized level she could possibly go home (even though they still couldn't name what brought her to the hospital in the first place).

That Sunday came. Knowing I had to preach, Donya insisted on staying at the hospital the night before while I rested at home. I declined because Tanndra seemed to be in the best mindset I'd seen her in the entire time in the hospital, I wanted to be around her. I remember Tanndra sitting up in her bed that night and us having a conversation like old times. I felt like I finally got to hear from the real Tanndra. Like last time, she asked many questions about why she was in the hospital. She was concerned about the baby, but I assured her the meds she received wouldn't cause any harm.

When morning came, I got up early to go home to shower and get ready for church. Tanndra knew my friend who invited me to preach and came with me to his church once before when I preached there. She hated that she couldn't go. She'd always supported me whenever I preached. No matter how far I had to go, she always traveled with me.

Our conversation that morning was even clearer than the night before. She seemed to really be coming back to herself. I held her hand, gave her a kiss, and told her I would be back after service. I remember leaving the hospital feeling as optimistic I'd been all week. Things finally looked to be on the up and up.

After leaving home from getting dressed, I was on my way to the church. It was a cloudy gloomy morning. About halfway to the church it began pouring down raining. It was one of those downpours where they sky looked like the bottom fell out as water drenched the earth. As soon as I arrived at the church, my phone rang. I didn't even have the chance to park yet. When I answered, it was one of the doctors from the hospital. She confirmed I was Tanndra's husband before proceeding to break some terrifying news to me I did not expect to receive.

"Your wife just had another seizure. This time it was much worse than the first one a few days ago. Our team was able to control it but because of its severity, we're very afraid of what may happen if she seizes again. No one was in the room at the time, but luckily the door was open where one of the nurses could see her and she immediately called for assistance. We're worried about her airway being cutoff if she were to seize again. To keep her and the baby safe by protecting her airway in the case of another seizure, we're going to place her on a ventilator. However, we need your permission before we do so."

I was lost for words. I could not register what I'd heard. Before answering the doctor's question, I told her I'd just left her and everything was fine. I asked, "How on earth did things change from us having a wonderful conversation three hours ago, to her now having to be placed on a ventilator?" She said the seizure could have happened for a number of reasons, but she couldn't give an exact one. I thought it was ironic how in both instances of Tanndra having a seizure, both happened in moments when she was at her best stage of progression.

I then asked, "Is putting her on a ventilator the only option?" She replied saying it was the best thing to do in order to keep the worst of the worst from happening in the event of another seizure.

I didn't like what I heard. A ventilator? Really? The first thought that comes to mind when I think of a ventilator is someone being on life support. I told the doctor just that and she assured me ventilators are used for many more reasons than just keeping someone on life support. She tried to make me feel better by convincing me Tanndra was nowhere near a life support state so don't let that scare me at all. The main task from the medical team's view was to be cautionary in protecting her airway and that's it.

I asked the doctor if giving them the permission was the best medical choice and of course, she said yes. Therefore, I hesitantly gave the okay. I then asked when it would be done and she said they would begin the process ASAP. I asked her if I needed to be there for it. She responded saying I could if I wanted to, but it wasn't necessary. I told her I was actually in front of a church where I'm supposed to deliver a sermon, but had no problem at all changing plans to head straight to the hospital. She replied, "It's your choice. Honestly, there's nothing you can do for her if you're here. Placing her on the ventilator will have her in intubation so she's not going to be able to talk to you and will likely be heavily induced from the medicine we're going to give her for the procedure."

I simply said okay and we ended the call.

There I was. Sitting in the car with my nice dress shirt and suit on staring out my windshield as the rain pounded loud as drums on the glass. I could not move. I could not think. It felt as if I was in an inimitable paralysis. I didn't know what to do. I dreaded going to the hospital because I did not know what my eyes would be in for whenever I saw her. I've seen people on ventilators before, and it just so happens that all were in life support situations. Even though the doctor gave me the assurance that wasn't the case for Tanndra, I knew just the image alone would prompt a haunting feeling for me.

What was I to do? Go to the hospital or go inside the church? As the rain calmed enough for me to have an unblemished view of what was in front of me, I noticed I was directly in front of the church in a parking space. That's when I observed the nice beautiful steeple on top of it. That's when I found myself being in a peculiar dynamic. I was stuck between a steeple and a seizure. I was forced to make this difficult choice between continuing toward the steeple in front of me, or turning around to go back to the seizure behind me.

At the steeple were people awaiting to hear the word of God, while at the seizure awaited a wife who wouldn't be able to hear anything at all. At the steeple was a place that represented hope, while at the seizure was a place that started to feel like it represented hopelessness. At the steeple, I would go in doing my best to stand strong and speak powerfully, while at the seizure I would go in doing my best not to stand weak and weep powerfully. At the steeple in front of me was supposed to be healing, yet at the seizure behind me was sickness. At the steeple in front of me was supposed to be peace, yet at the seizure behind me was chaos. The steeple in front of me embodied a miraculous faith, yet the seizure behind me embodied a mighty fear.

For what felt like hours I sat in my car with all of these thoughts racing in my mind on whether to go to the steeple to minister, or go to the seizure to mourn. Feeling so misplaced, I finally bowed my head and prayed to God asking what I should do. I then felt God's response say, "I have Tanndra taken care of. You go in the church and take care of the people. Don't worry."

With that response, God reminded me when we find ourselves in unfortunate situations we have absolutely no control over, the best and the only thing we can do is leave the situation up to the one who has control over all things. The doctor was right; there was nothing I could do by changing plans to be there. However, what I could do from my distance was rely on God's presence to be there with my wife in my absence, knowing he is able to care for her far better than I am. Moreover, the great part is knowing that when I arrive to be there with her, he wouldn't depart as if he's on shift. Rather, he'd remain there covering the both of us because his word says, "Lo, I am with you *always*."

I got out of my car walking toward that steeple and inside the church. I will admit I did not deliver the sermon with the energy I usually bring while preaching, but I got through it. Never had I found myself in such a position preaching while feeling so much pain at the same time. I believe a little of that pain could be seen, but that's not a bad thing. The people may not have realized it but not only did they hear a completed sermon, they were also seeing the beginning stages of what was a sermon in progress through my life. Sermons are just as much lived as they are spoken.

After service ended, I greeted all the members and gave thanks to my good friend Pastor Eric Vickers for inviting me. Still gloomy and cloudy outside, I drove off out of the parking lot headed straight to the hospital. I tried not to let my mind wander off into having a preconceived image of what I was about to see. Driving away, I could see the church steeple in my rearview mirror. The steeple was now behind me, and I was on my way to both a seizure and a ventilator ahead of me.

7

God...Why?

"No matter what precautions we take, no matter how
well we have put together a good life, no matter how
hard we have worked to be healthy, wealthy,
comfortable with friends and family, and successful
with our career—something will inevitably ruin it."
– Tim Keller

August 30, 2015

I drove straight from the church to the hospital. I
didn't bother making a stop home to change out of my
suit. My entire body had a sick feeling of nervousness
and uneasiness about it. I still could not wrap my head
around what I'd heard from the doctor just three hours
before. As I drove, I made calls to the family members
who'd literally just left two days ago to let them know
what transpired. It threw everyone off course. Just like
me, they didn't see this coming at all. Most of them
decided to hop right back into their cars within the week
to come back down to see her.

A few of my church members at the church I served as
youth pastor were on their way to the hospital which they'd
planned to do before the news of that morning. I texted
them to let them know what happened just to give them a
heads up on what to expect to see, even though I myself
didn't know what to expect exactly. They conveyed their

sympathies as they couldn't imagine such catastrophe happening to Tanndra. My update on her condition didn't deter them from coming. They wanted to be there for us. They wanted to be there for her.

They all knew and loved Tanndra. To them she wasn't just a fellow church member, but she was also a friend. She was always at the church helping me with the young people, singing in the choir, and volunteering in different ministries. In fact, she was just getting ready to launch a new ministry at the church about grief that we were excited about. She'd recently written part one of what was going to be a five-part series of articles for our church newsletter about the subject matter of grief. These are her own words:

"It is my belief that if we choose to be educated about this natural and normal response to loss, we can work through our own grief and also be better supporters of others who are grieving."

The irony of that statement lay in the fact that it was now our own family who needed the support during what could be viewed as a grieving moment.

When I arrived at the hospital, I did not move with the swiftness I usually did to get out of the car and go to her room. I took my time. I tried my best to prepare myself for what I would see. I walked through the entrance doors deciding to take the stairs instead of the elevator to get to the ICU floor. I made the long walk down to the end of the hallway where her room was located. Typically, I would peek into the other rooms on both sides of the hallway to see how other patients were doing. Since Tanndra's admittance, I'd familiarized myself with the faces and visual conditions of the other ICU patients. I would notice if someone had progressed, or declined, or went home. As I walked, I would also pray for God to touch and bring healing to each individual in every room.

This time my mind was too overwhelmed to look around the other rooms as I walked with a bowed head. This time my heart was too troubled to stretch my hands toward each patient to say a prayer. I needed hands and prayers directed toward me as my focus was only on one patient.

I reached her room, took a deep breath, and stepped in. There she was. Her eyes shut as she laid in an involuntary sleep. Her face barely visible due to so many parts of medical devices winged above and around her. The sound of a loud beeping noise came from a large machine that had a long tube connected to it. That same tube trailed across the floor over to her bed reaching her mouth. Her lips puckered open as the tube forced entrance into her mouth which made it no longer detectable externally. However, knowing it was still present in her internally suppressed down the walls of her esophagus was hard to come to grips with. Everything looked so uncomfortable.

I was not in the room long before a few of our church members arrived. The reality of the situation still hadn't resonated with me completely so I was able to interact with them in a composed and normal manner. Their visits shortly drew me away from the reality I knew I eventually had to face by the night's end

I'd made countless number of hospital and nursing home visits to church members and friends in my life. Whether a short or long stay, I just wanted that person or family to know I was thinking about and praying for them. I didn't feel like I had to go out of my way to do what I viewed as a small courtesy. I never thought too much of it until this particular moment when I found myself being the one visited instead of doing the visiting. For those next four hours, church members came by to sit with me, talk with me, and most of all pray for us. While some people may look at it as an intrusion, I look at it as intercession. I had God-loving people petitioning to the Lord on my behalf to help us in what was for sure a time of great trouble. I'd prayed so much over the past week that I felt somewhat empty, but having others speak prayers to and for me gave a refueling. I believed in what they said and most of all in who they said it to.

In between the four hours of visiting, I was told by one of the nurses that they were going to transport Tanndra to a bigger ICU room since she now had all of the ventilator equipment hooked up to her. Before taking her to the new room, they were also going to take her downstairs for another MRI. The nurse saw all of the company I had out in the waiting area and encouraged me to not worry about going down to the MRI with them. She suggested I stay and visit with friends. Plus, unlike the first MRI there was no chance of Tanndra being uncooperative since she was intubated, so I wouldn't need to try to keep her calm as I'd done before.

Some of our church members who'd arrived a little later wanted to see Tanndra to pray over her, but it was taking forever to be placed in her new room. Every time I called the front desk asking if she was in there yet, they just told me she hadn't made it back from the MRI. I thought to myself that the MRI shouldn't be taking this long. I then tried to go down to the MRI area to be with her but they wouldn't allow me. I grew a little frustrated because too much time had passed without me being filled in on exactly why it was taking so long. Finally, one of the nurses came to the waiting area to let me know they'd made it back from the MRI and she was now in the room. It looked as if she had more to say but didn't want to let it out. I supposed she waited for me to ask. Without hesitation I asked the question, "What took you all so long?"

She responded, "On the way to transporting her downstairs to the MRI area we had to make an emergency stop because her heart rate dropped down into the twenties. We acted immediately and were able to take the necessary action to get it back up to a normal level. We're not sure why it happened but because it did, we ask that you try to not let too many people come in to visit her. Even though she's intubated, we don't want to take the chance of people touching her or speaking in her ear to trigger another unexpected drop."

I was stunned. Even though she didn't say the exact words, the only understanding I received from what she told me was that my wife had been just seconds away from dying. I couldn't believe it. It added even more perplexity to what was already a great mystery. In a sense, I was relieved that I decided not to go down to the MRI with her because given the way I'd lost it when she had the first seizure, there's no telling how I would've reacted if I'd witnessed that scene.

By time they finally were able to set her up in the room for people to see her it was late. Only one of our church members stuck around and went in to see her briefly. All the visitors were gone. A few family members who'd made it in town, including my mom, didn't stay long at the hospital when they arrived due to being on the road. They went to get some rest and planned to be at the hospital all day the next day. Therefore, I found myself being where I was earlier in the day when I first stepped in Tanndra's room from church. No more visitors were coming to keep me occupied from what was in front of me. I now had to face it head on. It was just me—alone in a room with the only woman I'd loved the way I did for the past seven years as she laid there motionless.

I stood at the end of her bed and just looked at her. I looked at all the machines around her. Because of her intubation, she was being given Propofol (a type of anesthesia) through her IV. It hung on a pole in a big round bottle made up of what looked like thick white milk. I referred to it as the "Michael Jackson" since Propofol was the drug that he unfortunately overdosed on to cause his death. Yet another unwanted reminder that my wife, who'd just had a faceoff with death, was now on the very same drug that brought death to perhaps the world's greatest entertainer.

Everything seemed so surreal. As a man of faith, I've had multiple conversations with God throughout my life. In fact, I speak to God every day. As I stood in front of Tanndra I was getting ready to enter into yet another conversation with God. Except this conversation was about to be the most honest, real, no holds barred, bereaved, yet bitter conversation I've ever had with the one whom I'd always looked to for help. I not only needed help at this moment, I needed answers. I needed an explanation. I needed understanding.

I didn't feel like praying to God, I needed to talk to God. I know that we often view the two as the same, which was exactly the issue for me at that moment. I believe we as Christians sometimes place an unwritten rule of expectation on prayer in that it's supposed to be spoken with high reverence, holy rhetoric, eloquent vernacular, and extensive vocabulary. What I had to say to God was the opposite. I didn't want to start out talking to him saying "Gracious God in Heaven." I wasn't in the mood to use the traditional idioms of acknowledgement before getting to say what I needed to get out. I didn't feel like saying thank you God for this and thank you God for that before making any requests. To use the terminology of the kids in my youth ministry, I felt like "going in" on God and I had no regrets for feeling that way. While some may view such talk as unholy, my response would be "what kind of relationship do they have with God?" Because out of all the relationships we have with people horizontally (our interactions with people around us on earth), the most important relationship we have should be vertically (the interaction we have with God up above). Which means we should all have more interaction with God than we do our spouse, our best friends, our fraternity brothers/sorority sisters, our church members, our neighbors and beyond. Therefore, because we have this often-visited interaction in this most important relationship, being transparent with our feelings and emotions toward God should come naturally. If it doesn't, then that means we're being fake with God. And if you don't like people being fake with you, what makes you think God likes or wants you to be fake with him?

One of my good friends and seminary classmates Charles Watson visited me one day in my office at work and told me, "God is big enough to handle our anger." When we come to the point in our connection with God in which we realize and believe this, it takes that vertical relationship to a higher level.

I recall doing a youth Bible study once about listening to God. Anyone who's worked in youth ministry will agree with me when I say kids can ask the toughest theological questions ever presented. Some tougher than any church history or Christian ethics exam placed in front of us by a seminary professor. One of my kids asked, "I want to listen to God, but I never hear him. Does that mean He's not speaking to me?" I paused and thought to myself, "Dang it they got me backed in a corner again." I didn't want to give any old churchy cliché answer just to have the pleasure of telling myself I answered her question. I thought long and hard about it. I then replied, "In the instances you feel like you can't hear God speaking, remember that listening comes by both hearing and seeing. You may not hear his voice, but you can see his voice through the reading of his word. I promise that which you can't hear God answer, you can read God answer if you open your Bible." Little did I know that that same Bible study I'd taught to help them years ago would come back into my life to help me years later in my most deplorable situation.

As I continued staring at her, all of the sadness, stress, irritation, fear, and outrage I felt inside came through my words as I began my talk with God:

"God, why am I standing at the foot of a hospital bed looking at my pregnant twenty-eight-year-old wife in the ICU on a ventilator? God, why is that the nurse just told me she almost died as the beats of her heart plunged into a deep abyss it's never been to before? Why is this happening? Why is it that I haven't had a regular conversation with my wife going on two weeks? I don't get it. It's ripping me up inside seeing her like this. I'm only twenty-six. She's only twenty-eight. Why am I at the hospital listening to the beeps of a machine helping her breathe instead of at home listening to the sound of her laughter from watching an episode of *Martin* as we do nightly? I guess this is what 'In sickness and in health' entails. When I made those vows, I meant every single word. However, I thought I wouldn't have to back them up until we were in our seventies or eighties. She doesn't deserve this. She was just at her new job doing what she loves, and now after the snap of a finger she's in this incapacitated state. God, what about the baby? We're supposed to be on our way to Miami to share an intimate important moment together of finding out the gender of our child. Instead I'm doing my best not to even think about the effects all of this medicine is having on the baby. The doctors seem solely concerned about Tanndra and rarely even bring up the baby. Do they care about what happens to him or her? God, this doesn't look good. Am I going to leave this hospital without bringing home my wife or the child I haven't even met yet? Why is it that she's in front of me fighting for her life, when at the same time there's new life developing inside of her? God I don't want to lose her. Things were just picking up for us. We finally felt like life was working in our favor and coming together for us financially. We were ecstatic about being pregnant. The 'power couple' as many friends call us was about to announce what everyone always asked about. We were just planning on how we would make the pregnancy known to the rest of our family and friends. And now that secret and surprise is spoiled. Is she going to make it out of here? Is she ever going to wake up and be okay? How come the doctors still can't figure out what's wrong with her? I don't like this. I don't know what to do. I need my wife back. God, why are you allowing this to happen to us? Why are you allowing this to happen to me?"

I honestly don't know if I can say I was actually looking for God to answer me by responding to my soliloquy filled with questions of why. But He did. Still standing in the same spot in that ICU room at the foot of the bed, I felt something tug at the core of my heart and work its way up to the neurons of my brain. A particular scripture came to mind, and it was God's answer to me. As I'd told my youth group, I was getting ready to listen to God speak to me not by hearing but by seeing. I didn't need to pull out a Bible to see this scripture. It was one I knew by memorization, and was also one in which I'd preached from. I asked God why, and God answered through his word in John 11:4: "Jesus said, this sickness will not end in death. No, it is for God's glory so that God's Son may be glorified through it."

That was it. That was his answer to me. That what I saw wouldn't end in death. That what I looked at in front of me wouldn't conclude with a funeral. Rather, what I saw was something that God would get the glory through.

I grinned slightly which was aimed at God. The only thing I could think to myself after getting that answer was, "Wow, God. Okay. How can I argue with that? I now know why. For your glory shall it be."

I then moved over from the foot of the bed toward the front. I pulled up a chair, sat down, and grabbed Tanndra's hand. She couldn't see me, hear me, or feel me. But I was there and didn't intend on going anywhere. God's answer provided a temporary peace for me at that moment. Did his answer make things easier? No. Did his answer change my circumstance? No. Did his answer open her eyes or give her the ability to vocalize? No. Did his answer immediately make everything fine for me? No. Did his answer take us home that night returning back to our normal lives? No. But his answer did provide me an ephemeral peace.

One thing about peace is that it doesn't always eliminate or erase the chaos in our lives, but it can even it out, making it just a little less rocky. My chaos was still present, but at least on that night after seeing God's answer I was able to go to sleep knowing why.

8

Nurse Ashley

"We don't meet people by accident. They are meant to cross our path for a reason."

August 31 – September 9, 2015

Three days after being placed on the ventilator, the doctors decided to remove it. Tanndra hadn't showed any more seizure symptoms so they felt it was safe to do so. Because of the strength of the Propofol, she was still pretty much out of it. She would open her eyes and move her body a little. She could even respond to my voice by nodding her head acknowledging she could hear me.

Meanwhile, we were still at a standstill as far as figuring out what made her sick. After the multiple tests for viral meningitis, the doctors completely ruled it out. They then told me it could be Lupus. Turns out that was ruled out shortly after. They then suggested it could be Vasculitis, which I'd never heard of before. Once again, they then ruled that out shortly after. The entire medical team could see my frustration growing. I couldn't understand how on earth we'd been there so long but still didn't know why. There were a few times I got a little snappy with them which is totally out of my character, but I believe anyone would react the same way no matter how calm of a personality they have.

After seeing how serious things were when they intubated her, I decided to go ahead and let everyone know what was going on. I didn't go into deep detail, but I did post on my Facebook page that Tanndra was in the hospital going on her second week with an illness the doctors couldn't pinpoint. I asked everyone to pray for us and for the doctors to come up with the right diagnosis. I left out mentioning she was pregnant. I still held on to believing she'd recover from this quickly and life would return to its regular schedule. The only people who knew by this time, outside those we initially told, were the family and friends who came in to visit her. The baby bump was now pretty obvious so I couldn't have hidden it even if I'd tried.

One particular night, I thought my belief in her soon-to-be-recovery was on the verge of fruition. I remember having my iPad with me as I sat at her bedside. Though her eyes were wide open and her movements became more flexible, she still wouldn't speak. I decided to open my YouTube app to play some of her favorite gospel songs. As the music filled the room she closed her eyes and took it all in. I could tell she was 100 percent in tune with the music. During certain portions when the singer said a very inspirational verse she would smile and nod her head in agreement. She did this especially during one specific song we both love to listen to, "Broken But Healed" by Byron Cage.

"God can heal, He can deliver. Once you trust him, you will receive." I didn't know if Tanndra could fully understand all that had happened to her, but at that moment it was as if she knew she was in crisis and she allowed her strong faith to take over through this song to give her assurance everything would be okay. Seeing this put a huge smile on my face. For the next hour, we had our own two-person worship service listening to her favorite songs where she followed every word. This was a huge sign of hopefulness. Even though we still didn't have a diagnosis, as long as she was getting better I was fine. In fact, I didn't even care about finding a diagnosis as long as she went home healthy.

I felt good that night and it carried over into the next couple of days. Tanndra was now sitting up in her bed and speaking a little bit. When they put her on the ventilator they also placed a feeding tube in her which remained there this entire time, so she wasn't able to eat any solid food. She could only drink water and juices. One day her sister Donya had McDonalds in the room and Tanndra couldn't take her eyes off of it. She had the look of a pirate who'd just discovered the treasure chest he's been searching for. Donya could no longer resist her look, so she gave her a fry which the nurse was not too happy about to say the least. She and Donya had quite the exchange which was quite entertaining. I told Donya I would've given her the fry too. My baby was hungry!

Later that day, two of our friends came to visit. Joseph and Bianca were another young couple recently married—I was honored to be a groomsman in their wedding—and they were one of our double-date partners that we always enjoyed hanging out with. Both are also in the ministry which was another connection I personally shared with them. The three of us were in the room just talking. Tanndra was asleep. I told them how even though things were bad, I felt like we were on a route to improving.

In the midst of our conversing, Tanndra's body began to twitch. It then turned into an all-out fierce jerk. Her eyes rolled into the back of her head. Another seizure. It didn't even phase me this time. I called and signaled for the nurses to come in and just like the first time, the room was soon filled with medical staff. They told me I could stay but that Joseph and Bianca needed to go out to the waiting area. All I could do was put my face down in my hands, shake my head, and tell myself "Not again."

I was told they'd have to put her back on the ventilator, which was not the news I wanted to hear. I tried to make a plea for them to just get the seizure under control and leave it at that, but apparently, this seizure was as severe as the one she had while on my way to church. It was all about protecting her airway so I had to rest my case.

I did not want to see them do the procedure. For anyone who has never actually seen what happens when a person is intubated and placed on a ventilator, it looks painful. A plastic tube is placed into the windpipe through the mouth forcing your mouth to be semi-open the entirety of the intubation. They would also have to insert the feeding tube again. The type of feeding tube Tanndra had was a nasogastric which was a long slim tube pushed down her nostril until it was in the appropriate area of her stomach.

I returned to the waiting room where my mom, sister, some of Tanndra's family, and Joseph and Bianca were all waiting on me to let them know what happened. When I told them she was being put back on the ventilator, I could feel the energy being sucked out of the room. Tanndra's dad and brother had just been in the room two hours before when Tanndra was awake and had a good conversation with her. Everyone felt as I had that things were on the up and up. We couldn't understand how things could go from promising to painful so quickly.

My mom took the news very hard. She began to cry which created a domino effect for everyone else. There was only one thing we could do. We all stood in a circle holding hands and prayed.

The next day I was determined to force the doctors to give me some answers. My frustration with them was turning into fury. We'd been here for two weeks and instead of getting better, she'd gotten worse, and still no diagnosis. Even while on the ventilator her vitals still fluctuated to high levels in which they reacted by giving her a dose of Ativan. I felt like they were just treating her symptoms and that's it. I needed more to be done. I couldn't allow for Tanndra to just lay here for another day or for another week without improvement.

One of our church members suggested I have Tanndra transferred to another hospital. Perhaps the one we were at didn't have the personnel or resources to get to the bottom of what Tanndra needed. She told me to reach out to another church member who was a nurse at Emory University Hospital Midtown. Ashley Williams Gresham. Tanndra and I both knew Ashley. We all sang in the young adult choir together. When I called her, she was already aware of the situation. I explained to her all the problems and symptoms Tanndra exhibited the past two weeks and she quickly advised me to have her transferred to Emory.

I will admit I was not looking forward to all of the paperwork and procedures a transfer entailed. My mom had brought the idea up to the doctors before and they said we'd have to find a doctor who'd agree to take her on as a transfer patient amongst some other things. I relayed this to Ashley and she told me not to worry about a thing. She would take care of it.

I told the doctors my plans. They did not want me to go through with it. In a way, I understood, because even though I was frustrated and furious, I could see how hard they were working to try to figure this thing out. They were just as anxious to find answers as I was, it was just hard for them to get there for whatever reason. Once again, I couldn't risk prolonging the time as Tanndra was obviously not doing well. When they could see my mind was made up, they went over everything that needed to be done. For most people the transfer can take up to a week. Thankfully, because of Ashley, it only took us two days.

Little did we know that Ashley was making things happen behind the scenes. I knew Ashley was a nurse, but I didn't know what area of the hospital she worked in. Turns out she was a nurse on the Neuro-ICU floor at Emory. With all the seizures Tanndra had this was the exact floor she needed to be on if transferred. Ashley spoke to one of the doctors she worked closely with about our situation and he gladly agreed to accept Tanndra as a transfer patient.

I truly believe it was no coincidence that we crossed paths with Ashley through the New Calvary Missionary Baptist Church young adult choir. I'd always had small, cordial conversations with her, but never took the time to really get to know her or spend time with her family. Who knew the alto who sat in the choir behind me would play such a pivotal role in my life? No one but God.

It's amazing how God will place certain people in your life to be a blessing for you during certain junctures. That's why we must never downplay what we do or who we are. Many people feel like they have nothing to offer in life because of their vocation, education, or socioeconomic status. Don't ever think less of yourself. God has a purpose for all of our lives. That purpose may not play out the way we want or envision it. In fact, we may not even see or feel the fulfillment of it, but the fulfillment can be realized through the blessing you are or you give to someone else.

Ashley had just the right resources I needed to make this tedious transfer; resources she's accustomed to having and being around every day. Often that which we possess, that is so familiar to us, can cause us to view it as basic. Never underestimate the power of what's in your possession. No matter how long you've had it or how simple you see it, it can be the very thing that brings a miraculous change in someone else's life.

In the book of Exodus chapter four when Moses stood before the burning bush listening to the voice of God telling him to go to Egypt to free his people, God asked him the question "What is in your hand?" Moses replied, "A staff." This staff was something Moses was always used to having. He used it in the field while tending to the flock. Perhaps he also used it to help get around in his old age. To Moses this staff was typical, ordinary, routine, and served as a symbolic status quo for his life. However, God would go on to use that same rod in Moses's hand to part the Red Sea, to provide water out of a rock, and to bless an entire nation.

Just as all of us do, Ashley had a staff in her hand that God used to bless someone else's life. Whatever your staff is, embrace it. Believe in it. Most of all, use it whenever God opens up the opportunity for you to do so. Ashley, I thank you for making use of your opportunity.

The transfer was made the afternoon of September 9. Donya stayed at the hospital to oversee everything and ride with Tanndra to Emory while I was at work. She was still intubated during the exchange. That morning I had a conversation with the Infectious Disease Specialist whom I must commend for spending days working diligently trying to come up with answers. He told me I was making the right decision having her transferred to Emory and that he hated that there was still no diagnosis. He also informed me that he sent one of her samples off to John Hopkins to be tested for another possible illness he'd recently thought of. It was something extremely rare which is why he hadn't thought to test for it before. He'd never encountered anyone with it, but he figured testing for it wouldn't hurt since all other hypotheses turned out to be incorrect. Since we were leaving, he directed the results be sent to Emory.

"What is it called?" I asked. He told me to grab a pen and paper to write it down so I'd remember.

He replied, "Anti-NMDA Receptor Encephalitis."

9

Anti-NMDA Receptor Encephalitis

"In the spring of 2009, I was the 217th person ever to be diagnosed with anti-NMDA receptor autoimmune encephalitis. Just a year later, that figure doubled. Now the number is in the thousands."
— Susannah Cahalan

September 9 – 12, 2015

As soon as Donya confirmed Tanndra's arrival to Emory, I left work to meet them. Their staff assured me they were going to get down to the bottom of her illness and do all they could to get her out of the hospital and back home. They'd already read over her reports sent from the other hospital before Tanndra got there. They saw the complexity of her case, yet conveyed to me a determination to figure it out. I was impressed with what I saw from the hospital staff. Whereas the previous hospital had only one ICU floor, Emory had multiple ICU floors geared toward certain specializations.

When I walked into Tanndra's room in Neuro-ICU, I noticed her head wrapped in white cloth with wires sticking out. It was an EEG machine to monitor seizure activity. The previous hospital placed the same thing on her only two times her entire stay and took it off after about ten minutes. Emory put it on and planned to leave it on the next forty-eight hours to get a true measure of seizure activity if any occurred.

Although we were nowhere near being in the clear in regards to Tanndra's sickness, I was greatly impressed and hopeful with Emory Hospital's ability based on what I'd seen in just a short amount of time. People whom I told about the transfer spoke very high of Emory letting me know I'd made the best decision. They are one of the country's top research hospitals. Dr. Thomas, the doctor who agreed to accept Tanndra as a patient, filled me in on every detail of their evaluation of her after reading her two-week medical history and observing her with his own eyes. He mentioned that the anti-NMDA receptor encephalitis results would play a major part in what steps they decided to take. The results were due to arrive within the next two days.

I took it upon myself to research this particular form of encephalitis. When I read about the symptoms and effects, I knew this just had to be it. In fact, if this wasn't it, I didn't know what else it could be. Every article I read described exactly what Tanndra had gone through. She emulated all the signs from the beginning stages to the point we found ourselves in currently. The research was scary just as much as it was exciting. I thought we could finally put a name to her condition, but this was no ordinary diagnosis. If this was it, the doctors would have quite the task before them.

Those forty-eight hours seemed to take an eternity. My mind went back and forth about the results. One minute I wished for it to be positive so that I could have some ounce of relief in being able to verbalize what had my wife hooked up to a ventilator in ICU, and the next minute I wished for it to be negative because I cringed at the thought of my wife having this unusual medical illness. If I'd had it my way, there would've been an option C: winding the clock back three weeks earlier to when things were normal and none of this ever happening in the first place.

I'm sure I wasn't the only person fantasizing about that option on the floor. One thing about this ICU that's different from the other hospital was that the rooms were much closer together. There wasn't an isolated feel of exclusion like I'd been used to. Rather it felt like myself along with family members/friends of the other patients all had an unspoken connection with one another. I could hear their sobs. I could see their worry. I could feel their pain and frustration. And I'm pretty sure they all could see, hear, and feel mine. My life went from conventional to chaotic at the snap of a finger. I could only assume theirs had been the same. I wondered how long they'd dealt with their chaos. What were their lives like before being confined to a small square room looking at a spouse or parent they once saw be so lively, now be poked and prodded by strangers in scrubs? How fast did their heart jump every time a code call came over the loud speaker while at the vending machines and they could only pause and pray that the notice didn't end with their loved one's room number? What worst case scenario thoughts traveled through their minds as they tried their best to keep separated the optimism in what they believed, from the reality in what they actually saw?

I supposed we shared these unfortunate developments just as we did the small space on the floor. However, I must admit I felt compelled to be just a little selfish in placing my woes at a more desperate level above theirs. Because one thing we did not share was the fact that I had two loved ones to be concerned about. As went Tanndra, so went our unborn baby. Every time she got another injection, or another liquid medication shot in her IV, or another dangerous heart rate increase, I could not help but think about what possible damage it was doing to my son or daughter.

Those concerns escalated when the doctors discovered that Tanndra had several miniature seizures overnight in her sleep, picked up by the EEG. These were seizures that couldn't be noticed with the eye because they weren't strong enough to make her jerk or shake. Nevertheless, they were causing possible injury to her brain. In response, the nurses immediately increased the seizure medicine she'd been getting. I couldn't help but wonder how long these mini seizures had been occurring. Perhaps she was having them the entire time while at the other hospital but they never knew; this further reassured me I'd made the best decision by transferring her to Emory.

Every time I thought about Tanndra having so many seizures it was unbelievable. I just couldn't understand how someone so healthy who'd never come close to having a seizure in her life could suddenly have them on what began to seem like a daily basis. Maybe it would have been easier to grasp if she'd had one or two that the nurses were able to manage effortlessly, but the fact that it was the seizures that caused her to be intubated was just downright ridiculous.

Soon everything became clear. The doctor received the test results we'd been waiting for, and as my gut told me, it was positive. Tanndra had anti-NMDA receptor encephalitis. A very rare brain disorder so uncommon that most of the nurses were unfamiliar with it. It had only been discovered as recently as 2007.

I contacted many of our family and friends to let them know we finally had an answer, but that the answer was just the beginning of what looked to be a long battle according to the little I knew about the disorder. Everyone I talked to had to ask me to repeat the name of it over and over again. Just like me, they'd never heard of it. It baffled them. I'm sure it's baffling to some of you right now which is why I want to take a moment to let you read about the disorder yourself. The following is taken from the Anti-NMDA Receptor Encephalitis Foundation, Inc. website:

WHAT IS ANTI-NMDA RECEPTOR ENCEPHALITIS?

Anti-NMDA receptor encephalitis is a disease occurring when antibodies produced by the body's own immune system attack NMDA receptors in the brain. NMDA receptors are proteins that control electrical impulses in the brain. Their functions are critical for judgement, perception of reality, human interaction, the formation and retrieval of memory, and the control of unconscious activities (such as breathing, swallowing, etc), also known as autonomic functions.

Antibodies are an important part of the body's defense system. All healthy individuals produce antibodies against viruses, bacteria or tumours. Under normal circumstances, the body prevents production of antibodies against its own ('host') tissues. In some individuals, however, antibodies that target the host may be produced. When this occurs the patient is said to have an "auto immune" (i.e., originating from one's self) disease.

In anti-NMDA receptor encephalitis antibodies are generated against NMDA receptors and go on to attack these receptors where they are found in their highest concentration: within the brain. The reasons why anti-NMDA receptor antibodies are formed is not yet fully understood.

Anti-NMDA receptor encephalitis may be associated with a tumour, and may therefore be referred to as a "para (i.e., associated with) neo (i.e., new) plastic (i.e., growth") disease. If a tumour is found, it is most often a benign (i.e., not cancerous) tumour of the ovary. The most common tumour type is a teratoma. However, unlike other tumours, it may contain many different types of body tissues (including brain tissue!) A tumour is more likely to be found in young women who become sick during their childbearing years, and is less likely in very young (age 0-10) and older (>50 years) individuals. Anti-NMDA receptor encephalitis affects more women (80%) than men (20%). Tumours may be found in men. When these occur they are usually found in the testes. Other types of tumours that have been associated with anti-NMDA receptor encephalitis include lung cancer, thyroid tumours, breast cancer, cancer of the colon, and neuroblastoma.

The role of the tumour in producing Anti-NMDA receptor encephalitis is not fully known and is the subject of ongoing research. What is known is that most tumours associated with anti-NMDA receptor encephalitis contain neural tissue (tissue containing cells identical to that found in the brain), and NMDA receptors. It is presumed that antibodies are initially formed against NMDA receptors found within tumours, and then attack similar-looking receptors in the brain producing the symptoms and signs associated with anti-NMDA receptor encephalitis.

Tumour removal is a very important part of treatment. Patients who have a tumour that is removed, recover faster and are less likely to experience a recurrence (or relapse) of their disease than those in whom no tumour is found. All patients suspected of suffering from anti-NMDA receptor encephalitis should be screened for the presence of tumours. This is usually done with imaging (CT or MRI) of the chest, abdomen and pelvis. Women should also receive an ultrasound of the ovaries, and men should receive an ultrasound of the testes. Even after removal, tumours can regrow.

Therefore, people with anti-NMDA receptor encephalitis should be checked periodically for the presence (or recurrence) of tumours. In many people with anti-NMDA receptor encephalitis a tumour is never found. This may be because the tumour is too small to detect with imaging techniques, or because it has been destroyed by the immune system, or there is no tumour. In cases not associated with a tumour, it is not known what causes anti-NMDA receptor encephalitis.

What are the main symptoms?

• Flu-like symptoms
• Memory deficits, including loss of short-term memory;
• Sleep disorders;
• Speech dysfunction – the patient is no longer able to produce coherent language or may be completely unable to communicate
• Cognitive and behavioural disturbances – confused thinking, hallucinations, delusional thinking, disinhibited behaviours;
• Seizures;
• Movement disorders – usually of the arms and legs and the mouth and tongue, but may include full body spasms. These types of movements are very common in Anti-NMDA Receptor Encephalitis and the patient is unable to control them. They are often quite severe, requiring the patient to be restrained and sedated for their own safety and those of their care-givers. Sometimes patients are unable to move, and may appear like a statue, holding the same position for hours or days (catatonia);
• Loss of consciousness – The patient may be semi-conscious or may slip into a coma;

• Autonomic dysfunction – erratic breathing, heartbeat and blood pressure; loss of bladder control and bowel movements;

• Central hypoventilation – the patient may stop breathing, and may require a mechanical breathing machine.

• Vision and/or hearing may also be impaired.

The vast majority of patients experience a combination of symptoms and signs from the above list. Symptoms may come and go over the course of the illness. Rarely (<5% of cases), psychiatric symptoms (hallucinations, mood disturbances, delusions) may be the only symptom of anti-NMDA receptor encephalitis. Many people complain of flu-like symptoms around the time that their disease begins. The possibility that an infection triggers or contributes to the development of anti-NMDA receptor encephalitis is being actively considered in research.

Who is affected?

The majority of cases occur in young adults and children, although cases have been diagnosed in people in their 80's! Females are approximately four times more likely to be affected than males.

What tests are required to diagnose Anti-NMDA?

A diagnosis of anti-NMDA receptor encephalitis requires antibodies to be detected in the body fluids of someone with symptoms consistent with anti-NMDA receptor encephalitis. Antibodies may be found in either blood or spinal fluid. Tests on the spinal fluid are more accurate than those on the blood. Therefore, if blood tests are negative, the spinal fluid should be tested before concluding that the patient does not have anti-NMDA receptor encephalitis.

Imaging is an important part of the evaluation of a patient with suspected anti-NMDA receptor encephalitis, and should include studies looking at the brain (MRI) and studies looking at the body for an associated tumour.

What is the treatment?

Patients diagnosed with anti-NMDA receptor encephalitis need to be admitted to hospital where they can be monitored and attended to by a team of doctors, nurses and other health professionals. Although every patient's disease, symptoms and experience is different, most are treated with medications that reduce the levels of antibodies in the blood and spinal fluid. These include corticosteroids ("steroids"), intravenous immunoglobulin (antibodies collected from healthy blood donors that bind host antibodies) and plasmapheresis (PLEX; that involves use of a machine to filter antibodies out of the host's blood).

Occasionally, the use of more powerful drugs are required to eliminate antibodies. The drugs most commonly used to treat Anti-NMDA Receptor Encephalitis are rituximab (Rituxin®) and cyclophosphamide 9 (Cytoxin®). Many other medications may also be required, including those used to control blood pressure, stop seizures, ease anxiety, improve sleep, and to treat hallucinations or abnormal behaviours.

Medications may need to be continued after the patient has begun to recover.

What is the prognosis?

Although anti-NMDA receptor encephalitis is a serious life-threatening disease, the majority of patients who receive prompt diagnosis and treatment go on to make a good recovery.

Recovery is generally slow and may occur over months or even years. The recovery process is often complicated by many ups and downs, and by fears of relapse or re-emergence of symptoms. It is important during this period that the patient continues to be closely monitored by their physician. Even after recovery is well-established, routine medical assessments remain very important, including repeat imaging to ensure that no tumour is found. Unfortunately, not all people affected by anti-NMDA receptor encephalitis recover.

The disease can be fatal, with most patients dying due to cardiac arrest (stopping of the heart), or from complications associated with long stays in hospitals and the use of powerful immune suppressing medications (which makes people more susceptible to serious infections). Some patients may not recover completely, and friends and family may notice changes in the patient's personality or some other aspect that is different from before the onset of illness.

What are the chances of a relapse?

Relapses may occur in 14-25% of patients. Although no test is available to predict which patients will experience a relapse, research has shown that relapses are more likely to occur in patients in whom a tumour has not been identified, and in those whom were not treated with immune suppressing medications during their first attack.

Immune suppressing medications may be taken for prolonged periods of time (even after recovery) to prevent a relapse.

When relapses occur, they usually involve the same symptoms experienced during the first attack–although the symptoms may be less severe, and may not all occur at the same time, or in the same order as before.

Is it contagious?
No.

Is it hereditary?
Currently there is no evidence to suggest that anti-NMDA receptor encephalitis is hereditary. Autoimmune diseases may, however, be more likely in some families. Research is ongoing considering a possible genetic link in anti-NMDA receptor encephalitis.[1]

As you can see, this is a very complex brain disorder. Up to this point, Tanndra had experienced most of the symptoms like sleep deficit, dysfunction with coherent language/speech, confused/delusional thinking, behavioral disturbance, heartbeat and blood pressure dysfunction, seizures, and coma.

I was told by the doctors that from their research there had only been about a thousand cases of anti-NMDA diagnosed since its discovery. Being what many consider the top hospital in the Southeast, Emory had dealt with thirteen cases in the past. It was good to know that they were at least familiar with treating an anti-NMDA patient. However, as if things weren't already complicated enough, they ran into something very problematic with creating an action plan in treating Tanndra. She was pregnant. None of the thirteen cases previously treated involved someone pregnant. When they reached out to colleagues and other top hospitals around the country experienced in treating anti-NMDA

---

[1] http://www.antinmdafoundation.org/the-illness/what-is-anti-nmda-receptor-encephalitis/

patients, they could only find four cases where a patient had been pregnant while diagnosed.

In the medical field, it's nearly impossible to formulate a plan of action for treatment when there are only four cases to base it off of. Treating Tanndra was not going to be the typical protocol. If anything, her treatment was going to be somewhat of an experiment.

I was happy I could finally answer the simple question "What's wrong with her?" when asked, even though I would have to explain in detail when I replied "anti-NMDA receptor encephalitis" because it was a foreign term to everyone I spoke with. I wasn't happy that the answer I now had was about to take us further into the unknown rather than bringing us into the clear like I'd hoped. It was time to prepare myself mentally and emotionally for the lengthy, indefinite journey that lay ahead.

"The oldest and strongest emotion of mankind is fear, and the oldest and strongest kind of fear is fear of the unknown."

– H.P. Lovecraft

10

Trying to Balance Life

"Life is not always a matter of holding good cards, but
sometimes, playing a poor hand well."
— Jack London

September 13 – October 1, 2015

I tried the best I could to reestablish a regular schedule
for myself for the next few weeks. For the most part, I
worked my ordinary hours at work every day despite the
pushback from my supervisor and colleagues. They gave
me the flexibility to work from home or the hospital if I
needed to, or to not come in at all if I needed a break. All
things I truly appreciated and couldn't thank them enough
for. However, they saw me in the office probably more
than they would have liked. I explained to them me being
there was for myself more than anything. With so much
bedlam happening in my life, work was the only place I
knew I could go to for a sense of normal.

I must say that working for Mercer University could
not have been a bigger blessing than at that particular time.
I can't think of any other job that would have provided me
the love, support, and freedom to take care of family needs.
The Senior Vice President of Enrollment Management Dr.
Penny Elkins took time out of her very busy schedule to
visit Tanndra in the hospital and pray over her. Dean
Robert Nash and Dr. Karen Massey from my seminary

paid a visit to do the same. My direct supervisors Melissa Cruz and Kelly Holloway came to visit her and while there encouraged me big time with my struggle of allowing people to help me.

I was so used to being in the position of helping and giving. It was all I knew. I was quite uncomfortable being on the receiving end of help. I pushed back as much as I could when people offered money, meals, or even a break for me to get away from the hospital for a couple of hours. Melissa and Kelly reminded me of how many times I'd been there for others in their tumultuous situations giving my time and resources. They told me the least I could do was give other people I've touched and helped an opportunity to return the favor in whatever way they pleased. I finally conceded my stubbornness.

My colleagues at work Lael Whiteside, Artie Kent, Kelley Sinclair, Jaime Thomas, Francine Onyemaka, Dr. Michael Weber, Dr. Gerry Mills, Dr. Julie Petherbridge, and Dean Susan Gilbert all hounded me daily making sure I was taken care of when it came to having enough food and rest. I would always decline their offers, but I will admit that the food offerings were starting to entice me. Going back and forth to the hospital so much forced me to live off fast food for breakfast, lunch, and dinner. It got to the point where I salivated at the mouth just thinking about a good, fresh home-cooked meal.

I could no longer resist. One morning our church choir director Deborah Payne called to check on me and asked if I needed someone to cook me a meal. I was on the verge of declining as I'd done so many times before, but my stomach sent a quick signal to my brain to answer honestly. I told her I would love a home-cooked meal and that was all it took. She invited me over to eat that weekend with her family and I enjoyed one of the best meals I've ever had: We ate roast beef, ribs, chicken, greens, mac & cheese, sweet potatoes, cornbread, and cake. I ate as if I'd been castaway on a deserted island for years.

Though I strived to continue with my personal responsibilities and obligations, fatigue kicked me in the behind numerous times. Particularly while teaching my classes as an adjunct professor at Ohio Christian University. I considered going to the Dean to tell him my situation just wouldn't allow me the time to teach two night classes each week from six to ten p.m., but the tenacious person I am wouldn't let me do it. For five straight weeks, I spent Tuesdays and Thursdays working at Mercer from nine-thirty a.m. to five p.m., teaching class from six to ten, and going straight to the hospital afterwards to spend the night, only to wake up the next morning to get the doctor's report and then return to work another full day at Mercer. As the professor, I believe I counted the days till classes ended more than the students.

Donya was a huge relief many times staying over at the hospital with Tanndra on nights I taught even when she'd stayed the whole day with her while I was at Mercer. Because Tanndra was still in a coma and intubated, a lot of family members tried to get both me and Donya to rest by just staying home at night instead of at the hospital. I understood their reasoning—it wasn't like Tanndra knew we were there anyway—but neither of us could bring ourselves to leave her there alone at night.

One night after class when I arrived at the hospital, I was surprised to see a college classmate, Aftan Walls, in the room with Tanndra. Tanndra had been her RA during Aftan's freshmen year. She'd visited before and knew of the hectic schedule I had going for myself. She offered to give me and Donya a break by staying the day or night with Tanndra, but of course I was stubborn, unwilling to accept help, and told her not to worry about it. Aftan took it upon herself to just show up. I didn't know she would be there. She remembered the nights I told her I taught and decided to stay with Tanndra until I showed up. I couldn't thank her enough. She responded saying there was no need to thank her. She said even though I didn't ask her to be there, she wanted to be. I will never forget that moment. What I'm sure was a simple gesture on her part meant the world to me. It's not like Aftan sat with Tanndra laughing and talking with her that entire night. She sat there seeing her in the worst condition she could possibly be in. She willed herself to be alone in a tight ICU room watching someone she personally knew but didn't have responsibility over, laying immobile in a hospital bed. Aftan volunteered herself to share in our suffering.

It's one thing for people to hear what you're going through, it's another for them to see what you're going through. Aftan is an example of what it truly looks like for a person to be there in support and help of another. That isn't to say that those who aren't physically present in a crisis don't care or can't be a great support system from afar, but everyone can agree when I say in today's busyness of life, time is too valuable to spend on just anything. For Aftan to have used hers to be there with and for Tanndra left me in awe that night. It reminded me just how much people sincerely cared for us.

That care was further shown through various groups of people. Classmates, church members, my fraternity brothers, my colleagues in ministry, and Tanndra's sorority's sisters. Many of her Alpha Kappa Alpha sisters came to the hospital to visit and brought gift baskets, gift cards, clothes, and baby items. Their company, along with others, was a joy to have. When we talked, it wasn't just about the situation in front of us, but we discussed other things as well; sports, news, and memories from college. Just like going into work, it brought to me a sense of normalcy to help balance out the disarray.

While I continued to work and teach, one thing I could not put much time into any longer was the youth ministry at church. Prior to Tanndra's hospitalization I'd already planned to resign from my position as youth pastor at the end of the year knowing the baby would be coming soon. I decided to do it now. I cared too much about the kids and the ministry itself to see it lose spirit due to my limited availability. I helped my pastor bring in another youth pastor and met with him to give a rundown on the ministry. Although that part of my ministry changed, I did not stop preaching on Sunday mornings at various churches when asked. I was still being considered for a pastor position in Anniston, Alabama. Even though I was unsure how that venture would end, I chose to just go with the flow to find out.

During these weeks of trying to balance life with work, teaching, and ministry, the doctors kept Tanndra intubated. Crammed into all I attempted to balance was a very important day that seemed to come and go without much interest on my part. My birthday. Family and friends made efforts to get me to celebrate, but I vowed to do so only if Tanndra was taken off the ventilator. It was my twenty-seventh birthday. I didn't want to go out to party. I didn't want to go out to eat. I didn't want to go to a game or to an amusement park. The only thing I wanted for my birthday was to be able to see the eyes of my wife and hear her voice. That was it. That would have been the best birthday present I'd ever received in my life had it happened.

I made it clear to the doctors to do what they could to extubate by that time. They respected my sanguinity, but couldn't make any promises. Although the status of Tanndra's physical state was something I'd grown used to by now, I couldn't fathom having to spend my birthday looking at her like this. The previous seven years I'd spent my birthday with Tanndra. Whether it was traveling for a weekend getaway, having a bowling party with friends, or just going to Dave & Buster's channeling our inner kid, we always did something together for my birthday. It was usually Tanndra who planned it. I knew there would be no hotel stay, bowling balls thrown, or arcade games played this go around. However, just having the chance to look into her beautiful eyes and talk with her would have brought me such joy.

Unfortunately, it didn't happen. For the first time in seven years I didn't get to see her addictive smile as she gave me a huge hug and kiss and said "Happy Birthday." We didn't eat cake together (she'd always been the one to buy one for me). I spent my big day listening to beeps in a hospital room instead of seeing balloons in my living room. I withdrew from the slightest notion at celebrating. My dad and grandparents traveled to Atlanta to spend the day and night with me aiming to make the most of the day, but I opted to go into work the whole day instead. I didn't want to do anything. I didn't want anyone wishing me a Happy Birthday. I didn't want any gifts or cards. The only thing I wanted was something I couldn't have: my wife.

No matter how normal I tried to make my schedule, calendar, and life in general, it was days like my birthday that gave me the harsh reminder I was as far away from normal as Mercury is from Pluto. What was most scary about all this is that I felt I was developing a new normal for myself. Fast food began to feel normal. Sleeping on a pull-out chair began to feel normal. Daily doctor reports began to feel normal. Entering and exiting the hospital's parking throughout the day began to feel normal. And what hurt the most, being without Tanndra began to feel normal. I couldn't balance life. Life in its own sick, twisted way was balancing me.

11

The Decision

"Trust your heart if the seas catch fire, live by love
though the stars walk backward."
– E.E. Cummings

October 2 – 15, 2015

One thing that added to the doctor's continued confusion about Tanndra's peculiar case with anti-NMDA was that they could spot no tumor or teretoma. They'd performed a plethora of MRI scans on her pelvis in hopes of discovering a tumor or teratoma on one of her ovaries, but had no luck. In most cases of a person with anti-NMDA, a tumor or teratoma is spotted on one or both ovaries (or in the testes) which is the cause of the disorder itself. Upon discovery, the individuals in the cases then had that ovary (ovaries) removed and their health began to advance from there.

Because of this aspect, some of the key steps in treating a person with anti-NMDA receptor encephalitis include plasmapheresis, IVIG, steroids, and chemo infusions. Tanndra's doctors decided to start her with Plasmapheresis. According to hopkinsmedicine.org plasmapheresis is "similar to dialysis; however, it removes the plasma portion of the blood where the antibodies are located."[2] Because Tanndra's antibodies were working against her body, the purpose of the plasmapheresis (plasma exchange) was to take out her own plasma that had obtained negative antibodies and replace it with new plasma with healthy working antibodies.

This would be the first of about five different plasma exchanges Tanndra would undergo. They'd hoped to have her off the ventilator to do the first one, but they chose to go ahead and conduct it due to her disorder being diagnosed late into her hospitalization.

I cringed looking at them prep her for the procedure. Unlike the small IV needles they'd used to stick her in her arm, the needles used for the plasma exchange were massive. They stuck them in the juggler vein in her neck. I was sort of glad she was still intubated because I can't imagine anyone enduring that pain while awake, no matter how much numbing medicine given beforehand. Then, two bottles filled with what looked like cream soda eased down the entrance of her neck meeting her bloodstream inside. It took quite some time for it to finish. The doctors hoped for the plasmapheresis to do the trick in getting her on track to feeling better. They did not want to go the route of the steroids or chemo due to the pregnancy, but did make me aware that it may be a conversation we'd have to have down the line if things didn't progress well.

The first step the doctors wanted to take after the plasmapheresis was taking Tanndra off of the ventilator. To do this they had to slowly take her off some of the medicines she was on such as Fentanyl and Propofol. The plasmapheresis worked toward this goal momentarily. The medicine would be reduced, allowing

---

[2]http://www.hopkinsmedicine.org/transplant/programs /kidney/incompatible/plasmapheresis.html

her to move around a little bit before we would eventually hit a barrier with her vitals rising sporadically again. It was the Fentanyl specifically that helped keep her heartrate and blood pressure balanced. Once steady, the nurses would lower the amount of medicine again but the same thing happened.

The anticipation I had for her to finally be completely awake was indescribable. As crazy as it may sound, I actually missed her talking out of her mind incoherently and being physically combative in her gestures. Although I hated it for her when it first happened weeks earlier, by this point it would have been nice to at least hear her voice and see her ligaments freely move as they pleased.

The doctors' anticipation for her to be completely awake was almost as strong as mine, but for a different reason. Because she'd been on the ventilator for so long (almost six weeks now), it was protocol for the medical team to do a tracheostomy procedure. They explained to me how Tanndra had hit the time frame where the ventilator tube down her throat could possibly cause permanent damage to her esophagus if it remained there any longer without a trach. They needed me to sign off on it to be done.

The displeasure on my face could not have been more noticeable. They realized right away I did not want it to happen. The first thing that came to mind when I heard the word trach was the anti-cigarette commercials on TV where they have a person who smoked all their lives and now talks with a robotic sounding voice, and at the end of the commercial takes out the trach to reveal a huge hole in the middle of their neck. When they posed the request, even though I did not verbally respond in this manner, in my head I yelled "Hell naw!"

It was already hard enough to see Tanndra in the physical state she was in day after day with no progress.

Adding a trach to the picture would only add to the pile of visual anguish I had to endure. They tried to convince me to not be concerned and that a tracheostomy is pretty routine for anyone on a ventilator for an extended amount of time, but I didn't want to hear it. They could throw all of the logical medical reason at me they wanted, but at the end of the day, I simply did not want to put a hole in my wife's neck.

I refused to sign the papers. They urged me to do so for the good of Tanndra's wellbeing. It got to the point where they asked family and friends to talk to me about it. After giving it thought, I asked the medical team for a compromise. I wanted them to hold out for just one more week to see if something would change to where she could be taken off the ventilator so they wouldn't have to insert a trach. As much of a pushback as I initially got, they eventually agreed.

Another week passed and unfortunately things did not go in my favor. Tanndra's vitals could not remain stable enough whenever they lowered the medications again, so I had no choice but to sign off on the tracheostomy procedure. It felt like a punch to the gut when I handed the doctors the signed paperwork. I will say that they empathized with me. It's not like they wanted to insert a tracheostomy just for the heck of doing one—they also wanted her to improve enough to during the week to do without the trach—but they had to do what was in the best interest of Tanndra's long term health. Little did I know that would be the first of what was about to be a couple of tough decisions made in a short span of time.

The doctors had Tanndra undergo another plasma exchange since the first one had not produced the complete results they'd hoped for. After the second exchange, we still found ourselves in the same boat. That caused the doctors to take another step that they'd tried their best to avoid. In a normal case of a person with anti-NMDA receptor encephalitis, the chemo drug Rituximab would have been given as soon as the diagnosis was found. Once again, what made Tanndra's situation so peculiar was the fact that she was pregnant. Rituximab would be a risk to the pregnancy. However, because the plasmapheresis did not yield positive outcome, the medical team had to have another tough conversation with me about signing off for them to start the chemo treatment on Tanndra. The case they made to me was one that I understood and did not fight against as much as I had the tracheostomy. They needed to be more aggressive in treating her to help her get better before she possibly worsened to the point of death. Of course I was concerned about the health of our baby, but there was no way the baby could be healthy if Tanndra herself wasn't healthy. Therefore, it was better to take the risk giving her the chemo and just crossing fingers hoping that it would help her while at the same time have no effect on the baby. I was comfortable making the decision—until the medical team found themselves at odds about it.

Because of the various layers of Tanndra's condition and circumstance, she had two different medical departments treating and caring for her. One department was the neurological team which handled all things anti-NMDA which included the decisions of placing her on the ventilator, controlling the levels of the different intubation medicines, and going through with the plasmapheresis, tracheostomy, and now chemo. The other department was the maternal-fetal medicine team which handled all things pregnancy related. They came in daily to check the baby's heartbeat and to monitor the levels of medicine to be sure they weren't too high for the baby. They also did a weekly ultrasound to observe the baby's growth and development. They were extremely concerned upon finding out the neurological team plans to go through with the chemo treatment. From their perspective, the particular chemo drug Tanndra would receive threatened the health of the pregnancy more than the neurological team initially believed. This led to both teams coming together for a conference to determine a mutual decision for the best outcome. A decision that would then lead to me having to make a decision. The hardest unforeseen decision I've had to make in life; a decision no person should have to be faced with

The result of the neurological and maternal-fetal medicine teams meeting called for me to make a decision on whether to keep the pregnancy or terminate it. Both teams agreed that Tanndra needed the chemo if the goal was to save her from further deterioration. The consequence to that was the health of pregnancy being in jeopardy. So, it was up to me to make the call to keep the pregnancy and see if jeopardy would ever come into play, or to not let it ever get to that point by ending the pregnancy.

My heart felt like it slumped into an abyss. I couldn't believe what I was just told. I'd heard and seen these types of scenarios portrayed in TV shows and movies. I could even recall hearing stories of others about people I didn't directly know going through similar circumstances. Never did I think I'd be faced to choose between risking my unborn child's life in order to save my wife, or risking my wife's life in order to hopefully ensure my unborn child's arrival. The latter did not promise a healthy or sure arrival. If Tanndra wasn't healthy then that would directly affect the pregnancy anyway.

Unlike the decision of the tracheostomy, the medical team encouraged me to take my time in making this particular decision. There was no need to rush. However, if I did choose chemo, the sooner the better.

I did not want to decide either way. I didn't want to think about it. I didn't want to compare the pros and cons. All I wanted was for everything to be normal, which of course was impossible. I couldn't help but take a trip down memory lane to nearly two months earlier before there was ever a ventilator. Before there was a tracheostomy. Before there were any seizures. Before the hallucinations. Before the hospitalization. My mind wandered back to that special moment Tanndra and I shared in the OB/GYN exam room when we first saw the image of our child. When we first heard our baby's heartbeat. When she gripped my hand and began to cry tears of joy because the two of our lives joining together on May 18, 2013 had now produced a new life forming inside her womb.

That's the moment I wanted to go back to and stay in. With the decision looming over me, if I could have gone back to that moment and never left I would have. Just stayed in that exam room for the rest of our lives so that none of this would have ever happened. But I had to face reality. The reality was me now gripping her unresponsive hand having to decide if the image and heartbeat sound she cried over two months earlier, would be any more.

The hardest part about being faced with this decision was not having Tanndra's input or help to come to it. This was not only the most important decision of my life, but of hers as well. However, she could have no say so in it because she was still in this medically induced coma. Out of the eight years I'd dated and been married to Tanndra, there was not a more important time I needed her than now.

The type of relationship we shared was one in which we conferred with one another about everything. Major decisions concerning our household were made together. This was no doubt a major decision, and for the first time I would have to make it alone. The thing that made me feel worse about having to make this decision alone was the fact that it was a decision about Tannda's body. Although it would emotionally and mentally affect both of us, it would only physically affect her. My body had nothing to do with it. That made me very uncomfortable. It gave even further reason why I wished Tanndra could be awake for just ten seconds so I could ask her what she wanted me to do. What if I ended up making the wrong decision? What if Tanndra would come to hate or resent me for deciding one way or the other once she woke up and was back to herself? What if the decision caused conflict between me and others who thought I should have chosen otherwise?

The last question that came to mind was exactly why I did not share this news with many people. I'd been transparent with family and close friends about Tanndra's condition, but I only told about five close family members about the decision that needed to be made. Thankfully none of them tried to push toward a certain direction, or even offer their suggestion/recommendation for that matter. They knew this had to be my decision and my decision alone. No outside voices or influences needed to be a part of it.

I finally gave the doctors an answer after a week went by. The decision was to go through with the chemo and keep the pregnancy. I wish I could say I did days of diligent thinking to come up to this verdict, but I didn't. I even wish I could say I toiled and prayed every second of that week to come to the decision, but I didn't. I did a little thinking. I did some praying. But it didn't take much of either for me to truly know what decision to make. All along I knew what had to be done, and that was to simply let God do his work.

There are some things in life that's so complicated, confusing, and chaotic, it's impossible for us to think ourselves out of it. And this may be difficult for some saints to read, but it's impossible for us to even pray ourselves out of it. There are some things in life we're faced with where we must go deeper than leaning on rational thinking or pious praying to hopefully get out of the situation. In tough times like this, we have to have a profession of faith to believe ourselves out of it. To trust ourselves out of it. To undeniably guarantee ourselves out of it.

I had belief, trust, and a guarantee in God that when it came to Tanndra and our child, he would not allow me to leave that hospital with only one and not the other. He would not exchange the progressive health of one for the regressive health of the other. He would not allow the chemo to save Tanndra's life but harm the baby's life. Though things had gone so awry to this point, the fact that Tanndra was still alive was a sign to me that God would not allow her destination to be partial; rather, her destination would be whole. In other words, God didn't keep her in the midst of death to just bring her out some of the way. I trusted God would bring her out all the way, and that meant a healthy baby being brought into this world with no issues. God had already showed time after time that his goodness came through for us when we needed him. I didn't expect this time to be any different. Therefore, in making my decision, I valued and took my chances with God's proven record over the chemo's possible risks.

The doctors were pleased to hear my decision. They thought it was the best choice and were determined to do everything in their powers to make Tanndra better while at the same time keeping the baby healthy as well. They immediately started the chemo infusion once I gave the go ahead. As I sat with the attending nurse watching her administer it, I thought to myself this had better be the last big decision I'd have to make. I didn't want to sign off on anything else for special approval unless it was discharge paperwork.

Having to make important major decisions can be wearisome, bewildering, and perplexing. But it's those types of decisions where we must learn to sometimes sacrifice our own deliberate potency, and instead depend on his divine power to control that which we have to decide on.

"Trust in the Lord with all your heart and with all your mind and lean not on your own understanding. Acknowledge him in all your ways and he shall direct your path," Proverbs 3:5-6.

12

Rehab

"I'd rather be anywhere than here."

October 16 – 28, 2015

Things were beginning to progress a little for Tanndra. The Rituximab chemo treatment showed signs of working immediately. Out of all the things they'd tried up to that point, it definitely had the most positive effect. It allowed the doctors to reduce the drugs keeping her intubated without her blood pressure or heart rate rising. Because of this, she began to slowly wake up. Her eyes flickered open; her lips moved and she made an effort to speak although the trach prevented it; she was able to be mobile moving her legs and arms around in the bed, and she could respond to voice commands by shaking her head. It was only a matter of time before they would be able to take her completely off the drugs and remove her from the ventilator.

By this time, the hospital basically felt like home. I no longer knew what my own bed felt like. In seminary, we were taught that in order to do effective ministry and care for God's people, we must be sure to take care of ourselves first. Self-care is important. It was very important in my case as I was exhausting every ounce of energy as each day went by not knowing how long our stay in the hospital would last.

Five of my friends/former seminary classmates in particular forfeited their own time to visit me at the hospital on many occasions. Vinton Copeland, Matthew Brantley, Amanda Alexander, Marcus Johnson, and Tavonda Hudson. There were many times which they just popped up to check in without notice which I didn't mind. Their visits would draw my mind away from the busyness of hospital sights and lingo, into a place of enjoyment and fun. Their visits reminded me that although my life was currently engulfed in madness, I could still find a few areas in it to hide away in normalcy. In this case, the normalcy of true friendship. Whether it was having an awesome conversation about church ethics/principles with Vinton, sharing loud laughs that could be heard down the hallway with Matthew, being refreshed by Amanda's incredible pastoral care skills, or going down the street to eat some wings with Marcus and Tavonda, each moment gave me the essential opportunity to take some time for myself by taking part in something that exuded pleasure instead of pain. Even when Marcus himself dealt with a family crisis having both his father and grandmother hospitalized in the same hospital on different occasions for medical concerns, he would come visit me even though he had a lobby full of family two floors above. Acts such as these from these five, along with a multitude of other friends, helped keep me spirited enough to take on my own family ordeal.

Tanndra became more and more mobile as she was finally taken off the drugs that kept her intubated. Although they were no longer going into her IV, it would take a couple of days for them to completely be out of her system, then they would be able to remove the ventilator. When that day arrived, I couldn't have been happier. I'd spent about a month and a half looking at her with a huge tube down her mouth or in her throat—so much so that I got use to her looking that way. When they took it out, my eyes lit up as if I was seeing her for the first time when I fell for her looking through the glass window of the campus housing office where she worked. Despite some scars and the trach, it was refreshing to see her whole face. Her lips no longer partially detached by force.

Even more invigorating than seeing her face was now being able to look into her beautiful eyes which were now wide open. They'd been shut for so long putting her in a lonely darkness that I figuratively shared with her. As light reintroduced itself to her pupils, it reintroduced itself to the quixotic portion of my heart. For the past month and a half, I'd only been able to *see* her because of her sealed eyelids. Now I was able to *behold* her. My eyes could now be fixated on hers giving me a breath of relief knowing that the same eyes I stared into when I said "I do" were no longer under the threat of permanent confinement.

Seeing her face was thrilling. Looking into her eyes was stirring. But lastly, hearing her voice took the cake out of them all. It was weak. It was faint. It was soft. But just her attempt to project words from her mouth enthralled my soul. She was able to respond to words spoken to her. I kept telling her I loved her. Even though I couldn't hear her clearly, I could make out her lips moving as she said "I love you, too."

As many times as she'd said those words to me, they'd never meant more than they did at that moment. Some wives and husbands refuse to say those three words to each other due to being angry or upset at one another and they're not fazed by it at all. To those couples, I urge to you this: never allow the emotions of a moment keep you from using those important words toward each other, because you'll never know when you'll find yourself in a situation wishing you could hear those words from that person or wishing they could hear those words from you. I did not realize just how much saying and hearing "I love you" meant until I'd gone a month and a half without it, not knowing if I'd ever hear them again. So, if you're going to kick him out the bed to sleep on the couch for the night, say "I still love you" while doing it. If you're going to slam the door in her face while storming out the house to blow off some steam after a huge argument, say "I still love you" while doing it. I know it may be hard doing so, but it's better than living in regret thinking about the times you didn't say it when you had the opportunity if something was to ever happen to him/her.

Over the next few days, Tanndra's strength progressed. We were all surprised to see that she was able to stand on the power of her own legs even though she had on a safety belt at all times with someone helping hold her up just in case she fell. The doctors put a device on her trach that made her voice louder and clearer when she spoke. Cognitively there was initially some back and forth in terms of coherency immediately after the removal of the ventilator, but it improved as these days went by. I explained to her what we knew so far about her condition. It was too much for her to take in. She couldn't really understand it which was no surprise because I still couldn't really understand it.

Though her doctors couldn't find any tumor's on Tanndra's images so far was a concern, they were pleased to see her getting better. The chemo really did the trick to this point, and even though it was too soon to say with certainty, did not show any signs of harming the pregnancy. The doctors and nurses were so impressed with her headway that they recommended releasing her from the ICU to go to Emory's inpatient rehab hospital. I didn't think she was ready. It seemed too soon to make that transition and I verbalized that to the doctors. I still didn't think it was a good idea, but I capitulated to their suggestions since they were the medical experts and not me. Now looking back on it, I should have gone with my instinct over their expertise. We transferred her October 16 through an ambulance again. The nurses and staff at the ICU all gathered to see us off. We'd grown close to them over that lengthy span of time that they felt a deep connection to Tanndra and her situation. Tanndra kept mentioning how she was ready to go home. I told her our move to the rehab hospital was a step toward the direction of going home, but once we got there it felt like we'd made a U-turn.

On arrival, none of the nurses were aware of her diagnosis. They initially had her in a room with another patient until I talked them into giving her a single room to herself. I explained to them due to her hallucinations that still showed up periodically, it was in the best interest of the other patient for Tanndra to not have a roommate. Once we got settled in, I could tell a difference in Tanndra's demeanor. It changed from when we were in ICU to now. She was no longer willing to speak as much, and she looked very sad. It was as if coming to this rehab hospital triggered a sensitive spot in her causing her to shut down. That led into her reverting back to being more incoherent than coherent as she was days earlier in ICU. It was my hope that we weren't taking steps backwards with the disorder. One night one of the nurses became very frustrated when Tanndra didn't respond to commands or comply with being given medicine. I had to explain to this nurse that part of the brain disorder affects her ability to do those things. The nurse then asked me what kind of brain disorder she had and when I answered, she then asked, "What is that?"

You probably could have seen steam coming from my head. I didn't understand how on earth she was supposedly "tending to and treating" Tanndra this entire time but didn't even know what had her in the hospital in the first place. Did she not care to know about the medical state of her patient that night? Did they not give reports to one another during shift changes? Did it not bother her to ask me what's wrong with Tanndra when she's the one with scrubs and a nursing badge on?

I held in my frustration and answered as calmly as I could. I realized I'd been spoiled by the wonderful care and attention by the nurses at the hospital ICU and was disappointed to not see that same level of care and attention by some of the nurses at the rehab hospital. However, the doctors at the rehab hospital were great. They were well-versed on her illness and prepared a suggested treatment plan when they met with me. The plan included full days of occupational, speech, and physical therapy for the next three to four weeks, another round of the Rituximab chemo, and also a timetable to remove the trach.

The doctors leading the different therapy sessions were beyond helpful. Their patience toward and handling of Tanndra gave me hope that the three- to four-week plan could possibly be expedited. From studying her medical charts, they expected her to struggle in the beginning stages of therapy, but she actually started off at a more advanced stage than they thought she would. I was there with her every step of the way. While it delighted me to see her doing so well, it also brought me down at times seeing her have to go through the therapy in the first place. It was a reminder of how horrible things had gotten for us. I couldn't help but notice just how much weight she'd lost. Her waist had shrunk down what looked to be ten sizes. A feeding tube being the only source of nutrient intake for nearly two months kept her alive, but sure didn't keep her at her weight. Watching her have to reestablish the art of walking, turning corners, and going up/down stairs seemed unreal. Just four months earlier Tanndra and I were in the midst of our own self-made fitness course working out and running sprints together.

We'd gone from that to Tanndra having to learn to place one foot in front of the other while walking at a normal pace. Here I was with my young twenty-eight-year old wife in this gigantic physical therapy room where most of the patients were seniors getting help regaining strength after a fall or hip replacement. So many times, I shook my head in disgust thinking to myself, "She doesn't belong here."

Just when we thought things were looking up, out of nowhere she began to regress again cognitively. The hallucinations came back with a vengeance. Just like in the beginning of her illness, she was seeing and hearing things that didn't exist. Only this time she was fearful of them. So much so that she didn't want to be in her room. She sat in her wheelchair outside the room in the hallway terrified to take a step inside. Her heart rate and blood pressure began to spike again for the first time in quite a while. She also began to exhibit combative behavior again. She kept pulling at her feeding tube, IV, and trach trying to take them off. She eventually snatched both the feeding tube and the trach out which wasn't a pretty sight. The nurses reinserted the feeding tube but decided to leave out the trach per doctor's order since they'd planned to remove it anyways. The doctors were disheartened to see the setback. All of this led to rehab ending early and Tanndra being transported back to Emory Midtown Hospital.

Instead of placing her back in the ICU, she was assigned a room on the general floor of the neurology hall. Because of their familiarity with her, the nurses and doctors began to quickly do what needed to be done to balance her vitals and bring stability to her cognitive functioning. After being put back on some of her previous medication for a few days, she was much better. She was clear in her thoughts and conversation with myself and the medical staff. The doctors were ready to send her back off to the rehab hospital, but not me.

I dreaded the consideration of having to go back to rehab. It was certainly not my most favorite place because of the nurses. I felt that although Tanndra didn't complete all the therapy sessions originally planned for her, she did so well in the ones she did have that the rest weren't necessary. The only concern I had for her was her emotional well-being. She had a down and depressed bearing most of the time. I was ready to go home. Tanndra herself was ready to go home. She kept voicing that to me enthusiastically. She talked about how much she missed being home. I thought perhaps being home in a place she's comfortable and used to would actually prompt her to get better even quicker. It would put a smile on her face. Perhaps it was the elongated draining sight and sounds of the hospital that prevented her from being able to show any sense of glee. Besides as I've heard said before, a happy heart helps heal the body.

I made the request to the doctors to discharge her to go home. They were strongly against it. They didn't think she was ready and emphatically suggested she go back to rehab, but I would not bend without a fight. I got the social worker involved who'd been so helpful and beneficial to me from the very beginning. She understood where I was coming from in terms of thinking being home would evoke a positive reaction to Tanndra's emotional state which would then translate into positivity for her physical state. She stepped in as a voice on my behalf and convinced the doctors to contemplate my perspective. Though hesitantly, they acquiesced to my appeal and began the discharge process.

I could not contain my excitement. So many thoughts ran through my head. I couldn't wait to be able to sleep in our bed together. I couldn't wait to eat dinner at our table together. I couldn't wait to sit on our couch and watch TV together. I couldn't wait to resume baby preparation together. I even thought maybe if she got better really soon, we could head to Miami for a few days and still open up the envelope to find out the sex of the baby together. I still had not broken the seal yet.

It was October 28. Before leaving I was given a huge list of prescriptions to pick up from the pharmacy. She had quite a few medications she would need to take throughout the day and night. The discharge nurse gave me all these instructions on what to do if this happens or what to do if that happens. Home healthcare nurses would be scheduled to come to the house to check in on her. They gave us a shower chair and walker to take home since she was technically still supposed to be doing physical therapy, though I knew she didn't need it. However, I still took it with us. I didn't care. They could've sent us off with a hospital bed for all I cared. The only thing on my mind was that my boo and I were headed home.

13

Welcome Back

"Each day holds a surprise. But only if we expect it can
we see, hear, or feel it when it comes to us. Let's not be
afraid to receive each day's surprise, whether it comes to
us as sorrow or as joy…"
– Henri Nouwen

October 28 – 30, 2015

I made preparations for Tanndra's arrival back home.
I wanted everything to be perfect for her so I cleaned
our home to her standards. I made sure our bedroom
specifically was spotless because she would always get
onto me about leaving clothes on the floor and not
making up our bed. She was back to being able to eat
solid foods, so I bought groceries to cook one of her
favorite meals that night. I couldn't wait for us to relax
together in our own comfortable environment just being
us. I checked the channel guide to make sure *Martin*
would come on as always that night. It was customary
for us to sit together on the couch in the living room and
watch episodes of *Martin* laughing hard as if it was our
first time seeing it even though it was an episode we'd
watched twenty times before.

Not only did Tanndra's discharge make me excited
for myself, but also for Donya. She'd been a true
champion hanging in there with me for two straight

months spending just as much time at the hospital as I did. So much so that the nurses and doctors knew her on a personal basis and vice versa. I would often tell her she didn't have to be there and to go back to living her life, but she refused to do so. She was determined to stay there until Tanndra got better. She literally put everything she had going on hold to be in Atlanta to help me. I was glad that she could soon be able to get back to living her life and continuing her goals.

The night before leaving the hospital Tanndra was very eager to go home. She was still in a very coherent and comprehensible state. The best she'd been in since the start of it all. She looked forward to not having to deal with the irritations of the hospital. I could not wait to get her in the car. She hadn't been inside of a car for two months. When we left the room all of the nurses and staff saw us off wishing us the best. Tanndra was quiet during our walk from her third-floor room down to the ground floor exit. When she stepped outside she had a weird look about her. Honestly it was the type of look I would expect a prisoner who'd served a long sentence having when finally stepping outside the prison walls for the first time. She gazed at the street, surrounding buildings, and at the sky like a curious child. It was a chilly late October afternoon so I inched her inside the car where it was warm.

She silently stared out the window viewing the scenery of heavy traffic, Georgia Tech, Atlantic Station, and Turner Studios as we drove up 75/85 North. I was hoping to have a conversation during the ride, but I did not start an engagement of one and instead allowed her to continue her observations.

When we got home, I did not get the reaction from her I expected. There was no expressed emotion. No smile. No amusement from seeing familiar pictures on the wall. No friendly frenzy over being back in the home she decorated and organized herself. In my mind, I imagined her return home being one where she would hurry up the stairs, burst inside the door, run to our bedroom to jump faceplant in the bed to get a feel of a nice soft mattress instead of a planky hospital pad, sprint to the kitchen to grab a nice cold Sprite, hop on the couch, cover up with her AKA blanket, and relax watching TV.

Instead I got the total opposite. Donya was just as surprised. She had the same expectation as myself. We tried to amp Tanndra up to stimulate a buzz in her, but it didn't work. For the rest of that afternoon on into the evening she sat on the couch just looking at a random channel on television without speaking much. The spark and flare she had in the hospital the night before seemed to have disappeared. Donya stayed in the guest room to let us have some personal time and I tried to not let Tanndra's mood bother me much. I thought perhaps the reality of being back home overwhelmed her and she just needed some time to let it sink in.

I hoped she'd be more open by dinner. I sat her at the table and brought to her a plate of delicious steak, mac and cheese, baked potatoes, pinto beans, and cornbread freshly cooked by yours truly. She took all of three bites. She had an issue eating food while in the hospital. She would barely touch anything on her tray every meal the nurses brought her. We tried to push her to eat so that she could get back to her weight and also for the baby to get its nutrients. I figured she just didn't like the hospital food. She seemed to eat better whenever I brought her something from home or a restaurant. I was sure her appetite would be better once she got back to home-cooked meals and could choose what she wanted to eat. I was disappointed and a little frustrated at her for not eating. Before we left the hospital, the doctors strongly advised me to make sure she ate. I felt guilty as if I was going against their orders since I couldn't get her to.

Dinner unfortunately was a failure, but I had hope that watching *Martin* would be a success. We sat on the couch together watching two episodes, but she wasn't into it. She didn't give the erupting cute laugh I'd desperately missed and hoped to hear again. She still wasn't talking. She just had a blank stare on her face as if she didn't know where she was. I was fearful that maybe she was reverting back to an altered mental state, but forced optimism upon myself to believe otherwise. Later that night while preparing for bed I tried to get Tanndra to change into a gown or pajamas, but she just kept on the clothes she had on when leaving the hospital.

For whatever reason, she would not sleep that night. She kept sitting up in the bed just staring into the dark. When I could get her to lay down, she sat back up moments later. Sometimes she got up, just standing in place. When I called her name sometimes she responded and other times she didn't. She did this the entire night. She did not sleep at all, so I didn't sleep at all either.

The next morning I went to work while Donya stayed home with her. I clued Donya in on what to expect per what had occurred overnight. Donya planned to try to get her out of the house by driving them to get their hair and nails done together which was a great idea. Tanndra loved getting dolled up. In fact, the weekend before her hospitalization she finally got me to go with her to get a pedicure together. I was sure she would enjoy herself spending the day with Donya.

When I got home from work I saw Tanndra's car still in the driveway. I assumed maybe her and Donya finished up their girl's day out pretty quick. When I walked in the house they were in the living room. Tanndra had on the same clothes from when I last saw her. It was apparent they didn't go anywhere. Donya said she tried her hardest to get her to go but Tanndra didn't budge. She also wouldn't eat breakfast or lunch. I asked Tanndra several questions pertaining to why she wouldn't leave with Donya or eat, but she did not answer. There was no response from her either verbally or in her facial expressions. I could tell from the look on her face that she was drifting back into that mysterious mental place of the unknown. The optimism I forced on myself the day before was beginning to wane.

That night I cooked another big dinner but she would not eat. That night was reflective of the one before. She was on her feet walking around the room the whole night. She would not get in the bed. I didn't want to disturb Donya so I stayed up yet again all night with her. I wanted to go to sleep and just let her walk, but I was fearful she may walk right outside the front door going who knows where without me being aware.

The next morning I intended to call her doctor to let him in on what was happening to see what I needed to do. I woke up earlier than usual to cook breakfast for Tanndra before heading off to work. She loved my bacon and eggs. I would cook them for her just about every morning before she went to work. I thought if my steak didn't do it for her the other night, surely this would. It was another failure. Again, she wouldn't take a bite, and before I knew it she herself was on the floor. She got on her knees and starting crawling around. It was out of nowhere and for no reason. I just looked at her. I kept asking her, "Tanndra what are you doing? Why are you on the floor? Get up." She just looked at me with that frozen blank stare and wouldn't say a word. "What in the hell is going on?" was all I could think to myself at that moment. I knew then that she was back in a severe psychotic state and was hallucinating again. Where did it come from? I had no idea. How did it happen? I had no idea. Why did it happen after she was so much of her old normal self two days ago before leaving the hospital? I had no idea.

I wanted to punch myself. I realized that I messed up. The doctors were right. I should have let them take her back to the rehab hospital. She was not ready to come home. The rate she was going I could not wait to get in touch with her doctor to inquire about what to do. She needed to be back at the hospital as soon as possible. I woke Donya up to tell her I wasn't going to work in order to take Tanndra back to the hospital. Donya got dressed and came with us.

I thought once we got there it was a matter of going right back to the neurological floor to get her set up in the same area with the same nurses. It was nowhere close to that easy. For Tanndra to be admitted again we had to go through the ER. To speed up the process Donya and I explained to the ER team (who of course we'd never had contact with before) that Tanndra had been a patient for two months upstairs in the neuro-ICU and if we could just get her there they'd know what measures to take. They responded by giving us a long talk about protocol, which was their nice way of saying, "No. You all are staying down here to be checked out by our doctors first." We spent hours in the ER unit before being moved anywhere. All of Tanndra's previous doctors happened to be off or very busy, so other neuro doctors who were familiar with her case just from conversations with their colleagues came to check on her.

Tanndra had begun to become erratic again as we were almost used to by now, so they gave her a shot of Ativan to calm her causing her to finally go to sleep. As hard as it is to believe, this was literally her first time falling asleep in two days. She slept through most of the atrocious hours Donya and I waited.

I really wanted Tanndra out of the ER and on the neuro floor quickly. Donya and I tried to work our connections with all the nurses there to see if it was anything they could do, but they confirmed what the ER team told us regarding the protocol. After about the tenth hour of being in the ER we were finally making a move, only not to the neuro floor.

When we first got to Emory after the transfer from the other hospital, Tanndra was only three months pregnant. She was now over five months pregnant. Because she was being admitted again, hospital regulations called for her to be placed on the high-risk pregnancy floor this time. It was on the complete other side of the hospital. As we joined her in being escorted to her room, I could not help but be overcome with a controlled anger.

Here we were again. I thought this was behind us. I thought having to sleep on a hospital bed and couch was behind us. I thought having limited options in eating hospital food was behind us. I thought we could get on with preparing for our baby together. I thought we were days away from going out on a date. Days away from traveling to Alabama to see family. Days away from going back to church together. Days away from getting back to our normal lives in our own home. I didn't want to go to another room. I didn't want to have to get acclimated to a new set of nurses. I didn't want to go through weeks and perhaps months of seeing Tanndra's health change all sorts of directions.

We'd just spent two months being in ICU and little did I know after only being home two days, we were about to spend another two months in the maternity unit. Being home was just a tease. In fact, the hospital by this point was our home. It was my desire for Tanndra to be relieved and at a consoled satisfied happiness when she walked through our house door and I yelled

"Welcome back home!" I didn't get that. Looking back on it that was a farfetched wish. Instead what I got was the both of us being forced back into this grim existence of walking through a maternity unit door. It wasn't "Welcome back home," it was "Welcome back to the hospital!"

14

Congratulations! It's a...

"Having a baby is a life changer. It gives you a whole
other perspective on why you wake up every day."
– Taylor Hanson

October 30 – November 12, 2015

That first night on the maternity floor was a long
one. Tanndra once again did not sleep the entire night.
The nurse did not know exactly what Tanndra had. She
really just knew about the pregnancy portion. The
maternity floor nurses and doctors were going to be
filled in the next morning by Tanndra's neuro's team and
maternal medicine team who'd been seeing her. I
explained to the current nurse Tanndra's journey up to
that point so far and it left her jaw dropped. She had
never heard of the disorder and even thought herself that
Tanndra might be better off back in neuro unit.

The hallucinations continued through the night
which kept her up. She kept talking to herself as if no
one was in the room with her. Even though the nurse
did not know in detail the full report of her medical
condition, unlike the rehab hospital nurses she made a

conscious effort to understand it best she could and was very patient with Tanndra.

When morning came, Tanndra's old doctors came to check on her. They all had the same question for me when they arrived. "What happened?" All I could tell them was that it seemed as if she had a relapse of some sort. They hated to see her back. They knew how anxious and excited we were to get back home to return to regular life. Doctors from neurology, maternal medicine, and Labor & Delivery planned to work together the next couple of days to figure out what actions to take. In the meantime, it was concluded that Tanndra staying in the maternity unit was best.

Those next few days it was a challenge for me getting to know all the different new nurses. The challenge laid in the fact that I didn't want to be there. I was still trying to comprehend being back in the hospital eating cafeteria food when I was just at home eating home cooked steak. Family and friends could not believe the quick and unfortunate turnaround. My coworkers especially felt very sorry for me. Nobody had heard my excitement about Tanndra coming home the days leading up to her discharge more than they had. They were just as happy as I had been. It tore their hearts when they found she had to immediately go back. Our families were the most disappointed. They'd made plans to come visit and spend some time with her, perhaps taking her out to do some baby shopping. Our hate for this thing we'd never heard of before called anti-NMDA receptor encephalitis was growing intensely.

The doctors did more MRI scans on Tanndra's pelvis in hopes of finding some form of a tumor on one of her ovaries, but it was to no avail once again. They knew if they could locate a tumor then it would provide a solution to some unanswered questions still hovering among them about Tanndra's case. Some of them thought maybe the baby was blocking the view of a tumor in some way. Some thought a tumor was present but perhaps was not of size to be caught on the MRI scans. Others thought it was an even rarer case where a tumor wasn't present which was the worst possibility out of the three. It was the worst possibility because something had to be present to explain her relapses and continued show of symptoms of the disorder. The thought of nothing being present yet she still suffered from all the indicators would create even more confusion and inquiry.

Tanndra was pretty much oblivious to everything going on. Once she came back to herself from the hallucinations after a couple of days, she was unaware of everything that had transpired the past week. She couldn't remember being discharged, being home for two days, spending all day in the ER, or being transported onto the maternity floor. She kept asking how did she end up there because she noticed it wasn't the same room, same set up, or same nurses she'd gotten use to on the neurology floor. She still had questions about what happened in the very beginning stages when she first went to the hospital. The doctors informed me that the relapse likely caused some memory loss from recent weeks. I did my best making a long story short going down the list of all that happened to her from the beginning. She strained to understand, but it was too much for her to comprehend, so I tried to shift her focus on positive things such as getting out of the hospital again and finding a way to celebrate her twenty-ninth birthday which was just a few days away.

As hard as it was, I accepted the reality that we were going to spend yet another birthday at Emory University Hospital Midtown. Just a month and a half ago I had the worst birthday ever, and I was pretty sure this was going to be Tanndra's worst birthday ever as well just for the mere fact she was confined to a hospital room. As we did my birthday every year, we always did something special by taking a trip or going out for a night full of fun for Tanndra's birthday. This time would be different. However, I did try to look at it from a bright lens that at least for Tanndra's birthday we would be able to talk and interact with one another unlike my birthday when she was on the ventilator.

I wanted to make her birthday as special as possible for her. I brainstormed various ideas and came up with what I believed to be the best one. The envelope disclosing the gender of our baby was still sealed and untouched. Anti NMDA Receptor Encephalitis stole our plans of vacationing to Miami finding out together. It stole the celebration of my birthday and it was in route to steal the celebration of Tanndra's birthday, but I wasn't going to let it steal it completely. I made plans to do a surprise reveal for Tanndra as a birthday gift.

I took the envelope to Party City and asked them to open it without telling me the results. I then left for them to place either pink or blue balloons in a box. When I got back they wrapped it for me with smiles on their faces. I vaguely told them about our situation so they were happy to be a part of what we all hoped to be the first feel good moment Tanndra and I had in a long time. I anticipated finding out so much that I almost opened the box myself as soon as I got to the car with it. Tanndra had wanted a girl while I wanted a boy. Neither of us were headstrong on our wants; we would be happy either way it went.

Between thinking of the plan and going to Party City to implement it, I came up with another idea to ask all my friends on Facebook to record a short ten-second video of themselves telling Tanndra happy birthday and to email it to me. I was overwhelmed by the number of responses. My email box was full of videos of people expressing their love and wishes to her. I compiled them all into a slideshow on my laptop to show to her before she opened the box.

I couldn't wait to get to the hospital. During my drive all I could think about was seeing a huge smile on Tanndra's face once she saw what I had for her. Donya had spent all day with her while I was out getting everything together. When I walked in the room I wanted to bring as much positive energy in the room with me as possible. In the days leading up to her birthday, Tanndra's mood became very depressing. She kept her head down and didn't talk much. She had no belief in things getting better for her. She felt she had nothing to be motivated about and no reason to be cheerful or joyful. She scathed at the mention of celebrating her birthday. I knew there was a likelihood she wouldn't express much glee when she saw the video and opened the box, but I thought it wouldn't hurt to try. I had optimistic expectations that perhaps this could at least give her a temporary joy.

I went straight toward her to give her a huge hug and kiss jubilantly screaming happy birthday, however the jubilance was not reciprocated. I could tell today hadn't been any different from the days before. There were flowers, cards, and balloons that a few family members and friends had delivered to the room. I noticed she hadn't opened the cards. I asked her why and her response was minimal. She said there was no reason to open them because whatever it was she wouldn't be able to do anything with it anyways. Donya had tried all day to get her to spend some time outside since the weather was decent, but she didn't want to leave. The nurses, also knowing it was her birthday, tried to invigorate her throughout the day. Some of them even bought her presents hoping to bring her some joy, but it didn't work.

So it was now my turn. Everyone else's attempts had failed. What I had to offer was the last resort. It was the only chance left to see if we could get Tanndra to enjoy her birthday even if it was just for a moment. I told her I had a surprise for her. I couldn't help but kind of giggle because she gave me a look that said, "I'm tired of all y'all and these surprises." I used a video input cord to connect my laptop to the TV to play the slideshow. As she was watching it, I was watching her to see her facial expressions. There were none. She didn't have any reaction to it. When it was over I asked her what she thought but she didn't say anything. All she did was shake her head.

"What's wrong? Why are you shaking your head? Did you not like the video?" I asked. She replied, "I liked it. I just hate that people have to tell me happy birthday this way."

Her words kind of brought me down. She totally had every right to have that feeling. I probably would as well. Being stuck in a hospital room having family and friends wish you happy birthday through a screen when every other year you've been used to being able to be amongst them yourself to see and hear it said to you in person had to be tough to accept.

Since that surprise didn't work, it was now down to the last and final surprise of the day. Even though I'd brought the big box in with me, Tanndra didn't know what was in it. I told her what I'd done with the envelope I'd held on to for so long and that inside the box was either blue balloons signaling we were having a baby boy, or pink balloons signaling we were having a baby girl. I told her since we didn't get to share the special moment as planned in Miami, we could make her birthday special by doing it now as she unwrapped it. She asked me if I was sure I wanted to find out and I told her of course. I also expressed that if she wasn't ready to find out then she didn't have to open it. I wasn't trying to force it upon her. She hesitantly decided to open it.

I had Donya record it so that I could surprise family later on by sending them the video revealing what we were having. Tanndra definitely took her time tearing away the gift wrap. It was apparent she was in no rush to be surprised, all while there I was sweating in my shoes waiting to see. I had a type of excitement that hadn't been felt since before Tanndra got sick and we were going to baby appointments. In fact, I'd been so caught up in the busyness of Tanndra's healthcare that there would be times I forgot there was still a baby on the way. I had a sense of pride come over me that I hadn't felt in a long time. A pride that stemmed from the reality that I was a soon-to-be father.

So many friends and family members I grew up with already had children. Tanndra and I came late to the party compared to some, getting pregnant at twenty-six and twenty-eight. Everyone would ask me when I planned on having kids and my response would always be I wasn't in a hurry, but deep down I reveled at the thought of it. I always knew I would be a great father whenever the time came. From working with kids at the YMCA to working with them in youth ministry, I had a profound care and love for all the kids who I had the pleasure of coming across. I could only imagine how big that care and love would be for a kid who came from my own biological makeup.

I so hoped it would be a boy. If I had it my way, I always just wanted to have two kids. A boy first and a girl last. I imagined myself taking my son to WWE wrestling shows and sports practice. Us cleaning the yard together and taking camping trips. Teaching him how to love the Lord and love people. Showing him how to respect women and being just as giddy as he would be whenever he started dating. I wanted to have a girl last so that she'd have all of my attention in order to spoil her. I imagined covering her and protecting her to the max. Loving her so strongly and having her see how I just as strongly loved her mother so that she wouldn't have to question what real love was whenever she got old enough to be in a relationship. She would definitely be daddy's little girl forever and always.

The big question I faced was would I start off having things my way by having a boy, or would Tanndra get what she desired by us having a girl first. My answer was inside of that box. Tanndra finally got through the wrapping. She peeled open the flaps of the box and up they flew. Blue balloons! "There is a God!" I yelled humorously.

Every positive emotion and feeling in the dictionary could be used to describe me at that moment. I was beyond overjoyed, but it drained quickly away as I looked at Tanndra. There was no response or reaction from her. No emotion conveyed. I couldn't tell if she was happy or upset. She just sat there. I asked what she thought and she just shrugged as if us finding out didn't matter. She was indifferent about the reveal. I believe she would have responded the same if pink balloons popped out. Donya could see Tanndra didn't have the response she expected either and was surprised that Tanndra wasn't surprised. She left the room to give us some privacy. I sat next to her on the bed to get an idea of what thoughts she had going through her mind.

"This wasn't how we were supposed to find out," she replied. It was with that reply that I realized no matter how much I tried to make things special for her, it didn't take away the unwanted living truth in which we both found ourselves. At the end of the day, she still had this horrid brain disorder which completely flipped our lives upside down to the point where our 2015 birthdays would always be remembered as us being in the hospital. At the end of the day the way we found out the gender of our first child would always be remembered as us being restricted in a little maternity high risk pregnancy room, instead of a lavish Miami hotel room. At the end of the day we could only hope that Tanndra would be able to remember anything period no matter how bad they were since the disorder had already showed signs of disrupting her memory. That's when I got it. I understood why there was no response or reaction from her. At the end of the day, this just wasn't how we had planned things to be for us.

I went on to spend the night at the hospital with her. I was able to get her to talk about us having a boy a little bit. A few days after her birthday, another relapse occurred. After she'd been very cognizant and coherent, the hallucinations and psychosis returned. They were so bad this time that she couldn't sleep through the night. She kept seeing and hearing things that just weren't there. Whatever they were tortured her. It was clear that she was very scared, yet there was nothing I could do because I didn't know how to address it. In her mind, I should have been able to see or hear what she did, but of course I couldn't. There was a particular span in which she literally stayed awake for seventy-two straight hours. On top of the fright she had, the disorder had gotten ahold to the part of her brain that controls sleep function and totally distorted it.

The doctors knew this wasn't a good thing at all and were concerned that the lack of sleep could possibly cause more damage to the brain. Therefore, they took another major step in treatment. They gave her another type of chemo drug along with the Rituximab. This specific drug, Cyclophosphamide, was used in the more severe cases of anti-NMDA receptor encephalitis. It gave no more or no less of a risk to the pregnancy than the Rituximab so I was not as cautious of their decision to give it as I was the first time around. However, it didn't take away from the dreadfulness I had over the fact that all of these chemicals were likely entering into my son's system.

Something had to give quickly. I had a feeling that neither Tanndra nor the baby could go on like this too much longer. My sentiments were reflected by the doctors. A huge decision was going to have to be made soon. I didn't know what it would be, but I just felt that one was coming.

The next few weeks were critical as we would be entering the third trimester of the pregnancy by the end of them. I was happy to know we were having a baby boy, but there still lied an uncomfortable knot in my stomach because the question I had was would my baby boy make it through this pregnancy alive and healthy? And just as important, would my wife make it through this brain disorder alive and healthy?

15

The Countdown

"The best things in life are often waiting for you at the
exit ramp of your comfort zone."
— Karen Salmansohn

November 13 – 30, 2015

The hallucinations didn't completely go away after
the Rituximab and Cyclophosphamide chemo infusions,
but they did lessen. Sometimes Tanndra would clearly be
in her right mind, and other times she was mentally in
another stratosphere. There was no consistency either
way which became frustrating. Some days she would
hold a logical conversation with me all morning during
breakfast, but back to talking to herself as if I wasn't
present in the room by time dinner came. Even though
they hated it so much for her, the nurses had gotten use
to the back and forth of her cognitive state. Just like the
neurology nurses, they too had fallen in love with
Tanndra and wished so badly for her immediate healing.
They waited for answers to solve the problem just as
myself and the doctors did. We all wanted a solution to
stop this. We all just wanted things to get better.

Tanndra was due to have another chemo infusion in
a month. The treatment plan for people with anti-
NMDA in the early stages, calls for them to have
monthly infusions to kill the negative antibodies. In

another month, it would be time for Tanndra's fourth infusion. The maternity doctors did not like the thought of another infusion while pregnant; three was already too many for their liking. The neuro doctors felt the same way. Each infusion produced a greater risk. After conferring with each other the consensus was made that something else had to be done. They did not foresee Tanndra getting another infusion with the baby. It was just too dangerous. That left only one possible compromise: the delivery of the baby would have to come early by C-section.

They brought the proposal to my attention. The plan was to wait another three weeks when Tanndra hit the twenty-eight-week mark of her pregnancy to do the procedure. Even though Tanndra's health was not progressing as they'd like, they felt content enough with her current state to wait a few weeks before doing the C-section. She was not in a critical state in which an emergency procedure was needed immediately. The decision to do it at twenty-eight weeks was made because it's at that stage that the baby had a good chance of survival if brought early.

They definitely knocked me out of my socks when they came to me with their blueprint. It made total sense. I just had never thought of that ever having to be an option. In my mind, I still anticipated a regular normal vaginal full-term birth around the end of February. We were just in the second week of November. It would undoubtedly be an early Christmas present that I wouldn't mind letting sit under the tree for another few months before opening. I'd mentally, emotionally, and fiscally prepared myself for a baby in late February. All of a sudden hearing he would be here in early December was nerve-wracking. It put me on edge, but I knew it had to be done. There was really no other option. The only question and concern I had was the chance of both surviving and being healthy.

When I interned as a hospital chaplain in seminary I did my clinical hours on the Women's Services floor. I knew all too well about babies having to be delivered early for various reasons. I also unfortunately knew all too well that those deliveries didn't always have happy endings. I entered many rooms of crying grieving mothers and fathers holding on to a stillborn or post-delivery deceased baby they'd just lost after an early birth or C-section. It wasn't a good sight. I could literally feel their pain enter the core of my being as I attempted to be a listening ear while they expressed their anger and sadness in their own way. Even though the doctors felt confident everything would be okay with our baby, I wanted to prepare myself for either outcome just in case.

Our countdown was on. In three weeks, we were going to have a baby. Tanndra could not quite fathom the news. She honestly had no clue to what the doctors told us. Even when I tried to explain it to her in novice terms she couldn't grasp it which was hard because I really wanted to have serious discourse with her about it. I shared the news with family, friends, and coworkers. They were just as shocked as I had been.

I continued going to work the entire time up to this point. I was now spending more time working from the office than working from a remote place whether it was at the hospital or at home. My job truly took care of me with immense support. It stretched beyond the people I worked with directly. Everyday there was a call or an email from someone in another department checking on me. We were in the midst of switching over to a new student services system that all admissions personnel from different programs had to become familiar with. We had two prior meetings to be trained. Another meeting was scheduled that required our presence. Our director sent a mass email to everyone giving reminders. Right before the start of the meeting one of my coworkers came into the office to ask a question about putting an online information webinar together. I gave him a quick tutorial before we both realized we were a minute late for the meeting. We left my office to head there and when I entered the doors I was met with a gigantic bombshell. The room was full of blue ribbons and balloons. The tables were decorated with blue adornments. All my coworkers from various departments and even a few of my seminary professors looked at me with smiles on their faces. As I stopped in my tracks at the scene, they all loudly screamed "Surprise!"

It was a surprise baby shower and I did not see it coming at all. My coworker who I just gave a tutorial to was in on it as well as he slipped from behind me to join the others. Come to find out he intentionally came to my office to hold me up while the others got the room together for him to walk me in. There was never a training meeting to begin with. It was all set up to make me believe there was. Our director included me on the mass email reminders about the meeting to make me think that's what I was coming to, but she had sent another mass email without me copied on it to let everyone know what the plan was. They got me good.

They sat me down in the middle of the room and made me open each gift. There were so many clothes, blankets, and gift cards. I thought I would never get through the pile. Someone stood over me writing to match names with gifts so that I could know who gave what. It did feel pretty awkward. I'd been to baby showers in the past and knew traditionally where I sat was meant for the mother. I jokingly changed the name of our gathering from "baby shower" to "man shower." After I got through the gifts everyone went around the room telling me how proud they were of me for handling such a tough situation as well as I did. They expressed their love and continued prayers and wished the best in the upcoming weeks. I became engulfed with emotion. Their words kind of made me misty eyed. I couldn't believe they'd took that much time and effort to do something that special just for me.

I couldn't thank them enough. Every time I mentioned how they shouldn't have done it, the response was that I deserved it. They attributed it to the person I was and had always been even before our circumstance occurred. I'd always done everything I could to treat everyone right and with respect. Not with the expectations to receive anything in return, but just because I believe that's the obligation of every human. Even though I never expected anything in return, it was moments such as this that reminded me that how we treat others in life rewards us whether we want it or not. I left work that day knowing without a doubt I worked with the best people on the planet. I couldn't think of another employer who would have taken such sweeping exertion to pull off what they had did for me. That day was the first time I held a genuine meaningful smile not only on my face, but more significantly in my heart since Tanndra became sick.

I wish I could have transferred that same feeling to Tanndra in the hospital. She continued to show no improvement, going through the days being sad and down. Thanksgiving was coming the following week which I did not look forward to at all; yet another special day spent in the hospital. Both our birthdays and now Thanksgiving which was a holiday we always spent in Alabama to be with family. Even though I know how to cook well, when it comes to old-fashioned Thanksgiving food I leave it up to my mom and grandmothers. Even though they're some of my favorites, I don't know how to cook a turkey, make cornbread dressing, or bake a ham. That's why I always looked forward to going home for Thanksgiving to get as many servings of them as possible since I only got to eat it twice a year with Christmas included.

My mom, stepdad, and sister traveled to Atlanta to spend Thanksgiving with us. Mom came up with the idea to cook food at our house and bring it to the hospital so that we could all eat together. We reserved one of the classrooms the nurses did training at to eat in. My mom prepared quite the feast. It was a much needed relief since I was still mostly eating fast food while on the go back and forth from the hospital. We thought it would cheer Tanndra a little bit to see all the food laid out on the table. She had often complained about her dislike of the hospital food brought to her every day for breakfast, lunch, and dinner. I did my best to cook as frequently as I could to bring her something home cooked. We set up the classroom to look homey in hopes Tanndra would enjoy the day.

She did not want to leave her room. Everyone was waiting for her to come out so we could eat, but she refused to. My mom and Donya then took their turn at trying to get her out but she refused. Just like her birthday, she didn't want to do much celebrating this day. Even though she still battled with the coming and going of cognitive incoherency, she was aware enough to recognize this was not the ideal way to have Thanksgiving dinner. It made her sad to think that for the first time in her life, she wasn't able to see and spend time with her family on a day in which they all got together at her grandfather's house to have a good time. She missed it. It hurt me just as much as it hurt her to realize that. Tanndra loved spending time with her family; in fact, she's the orchestrator of family time. She was usually the one who gave out plans to everyone telling them what time to be there and what to bring. It was hard to deal with the reality that she'd gone from being that person, to being this person stuck in a hospital with all these issues having no indication of how it came or when it would end.

We finally got her to come out. She didn't speak to anyone, she barely ate anything, and after about ten minutes being there she got up to walk back to her room. That was it. Thanksgiving dinner at the table together was over. It turned out to not be much of a festive day. The Dallas Cowboys also lost so that didn't make things better.

After those plans flopped I couldn't wait for the next two weeks to be over with to get to the C-section. I was still shaking in my shoes nervously thinking about the birth, but I could no longer take seeing Tanndra like this. I wanted her to get back to herself. I needed her to get healthier. I hoped that the doctor's strategy to go in more aggressively with the treatment after the delivery of the baby would show instant results.

Being the ambitious motivated person she is, my mom had one more objective up her sleeve. The week before the C-section, she wanted me to gather our friends and church members in Atlanta together to do a baby shower for Tanndra at the hospital. We reserved the classroom again to hold it in. I was not sold on it because Tanndra hadn't responded to anything we'd done for her, but my mom really wanted to go forth with it so I helped make it happen.

About twenty-five people showed up with gifts anxious to see Tanndra. Some of them hadn't seen her since she got sick, while others last saw her when she was on the ventilator. They wanted to love on her and let her know how glad they were to see her. Donya spent the day doing Tanndra's hair and makeup. Just like Thanksgiving, it was a struggle getting her to come out of the room but we made it happen. I have to give it up to my mom and Donya. They did a wonderful job with the decorations, food, and games. It ended up being an entertaining night. The only disappointing thing about it was that everyone had fun except Tanndra. She did not speak to anyone. She did not help me open any gifts. She was honestly zoned out and everyone could notice it. Unlike Thanksgiving, it had nothing to do with her being rebellious by not wanting to be there. Although she wasn't talking to herself or hallucinating in the way I was used to seeing, she obviously wasn't all the way there. Whatever was going on in her brain had her spaced out big time. She was there with us physically, but that was it. Psychologically she was in another realm. Just like my "man shower" at work, I felt I was basically by myself.

It hit me later in the night that the baby shower was our last chance of possibly having a gratifying pregnancy moment together. We were a week away from having a baby and the only memory we would be left with was an appointment at two-and-a-half months hearing a heartbeat. To be candid, I grew very angry and upset at that thought. I couldn't believe we missed out on everything. Before Tanndra got sick I could remember us having conversations about all the things we planned to do over the next seven months to get ready for the birth, but it was all taken away from us. What made me even more heated was when I thought about it from Tanndra's perspective. I hated it more for her than anything. She didn't deserve to miss out on any of this. She'd always looked forward to the joy of having a baby, but all she'd experienced thus far was pain and unfairness.

We missed out on the happiness that is bringing a baby into the world together. We missed out on telling our family and friends we were pregnant in the way we wanted. We missed out on taking pregnancy pictures. We missed out on transitioning our guestroom/office at home into a baby room. We missed out on sharing that special moment finding out if we were having a boy or a girl. We missed out on doing a gender reveal party for those close to us. We missed out on walking through the mall randomly picking up a newborn outfit because of what was to come. We missed out on having conventional baby showers. We missed out on going shopping to purchase clothes, a stroller, a car seat, a crib, and all the other necessities. We missed out on going to our university's homecoming reuniting with friends proudly displaying our baby bump. We missed out on the excitement of going to appointments to look at ultrasounds. We missed out on the countless nights we could have had laying in our bed holding each other tight conversing about the future of our family of three.

We were about to miss out on going a full term 40 weeks of pregnancy. We were about to miss out on the opportunity of rushing to the hospital after her water broke and playing the waiting game as she dilated. We were about to miss out on everything I imagined having my first baby would be like ever since I was young. The feeling I had thinking about all of this sucked. So many things that can easily be taken for granted while pregnant I would have done anything for just to experience a few. Just a photoshoot. Just one ultrasound appointment. Just one shopping outing.

I swiftly gathered myself together because the more I dwelled on it the more I felt like I was about to slip into a daze like Tanndra. Now was not the time to do such a thing. I needed to be strong this next week to prepare for the big day. Tanndra needed me more than ever at this time and I was determined to be there for her doing what I could to make things easy to understand as possible. She still had no full comprehension of what she was getting ready to go through with the C-section. The wait was almost over. The countdown was almost finished. Life was about to change in a huge way in a few more days.

16

Accepting God's Plan

"Where you are today is no accident. God is using the situation you are in right now to shape you and prepare you for the place He wants to bring you into tomorrow. Trust Him with His plan even if you don't understand it."

December 1, 2015

Two days before the delivery we had one last meeting with the doctors. It was a meeting they'd set up after conferring together themselves about a number of proposed conclusions concerning Tanndra's case. A few more MRI scans had taken place, but there was still no tumor visibly present. Their study and research of other cases led them to believe that there had to be a tumor of some form causing the continued symptoms Tanndra displayed. Their research showed in other cases women experiencing the same symptoms had a tumor attached to one or both ovaries. The next step in their cases called for doctors to surgically remove the ovary or ovaries. Most of the women made a quick drastic improvement in their health once the ovary was taken out.

Those findings are what led the doctors to calling this important meeting with us. Once again, they had to share news we did not want to hear. Tanndra perfectly reflected other cases of anti-NMDA receptor encephalitis in which a tumor was attached to an ovary. Even though the MRI scans did not show it, the doctors determined the probability that one had to be there. To them it was reasonable to assume that the tumor was too microscopic to see on any of the scans. Even though small in size, it still had the capability to cause just as much damage as a normal sized tumor. That was already obvious due to how cruel the disorder had been to Tanndra thus far.

With all those factors in mind, the doctors presented to us their combined approach on how to go about solving the issue. Since they were already going to have Tanndra surgically open for the C-section, they wanted to go ahead and remove both of her ovaries at the same time as well. Because the tumor was assumed to be too small there was no way they could play a guessing game as to which ovary it was on. Therefore, in their view removing both was the only option because it guaranteed the source of the problem being eradicated.

As neophyte as I was when it came to knowing about the female reproductive process, one of the few things I did know was that without the ovaries women are not able have children. The look on my face spoke two words again as it had before. "Hell naw!" There had to be another alternative. There had to be another option. I couldn't just say okay to what they proposed and go on like it didn't matter. We'd always wanted more than one child. I know we were in a troublesome situation at the moment, but that didn't mean a future didn't exist for us. Never did I think this disorder was going to keep Tanndra down and out forever. I was hopeful things would return to normal eventually.

I attempted to suggest routes other than the one presented as a way to go. Perhaps they could leave both ovaries in for the time being and see what more aggressive treatment would do after the baby was here?

Their counter was that the treatment would only temporarily solve issues and that the ovaries needed to be removed to solve the issue altogether for the long term.

Perhaps they could leave both ovaries in for the time being and keep doing the scans until they could hopefully locate which ovary the tumor was on? Their counter was that Tanndra had already gone through enough. Surgically opening her up for the C-section, closing her up, and then going right back to opening her up again would be too much on her. Plus, at this point the only way the tumor would be picked up from a scan after the C-section was if it grew and that was certainly not worth taking the risk.

Perhaps once they started the surgery and took an up-close look they would spot which ovary the tumor was on and just remove it instead of both. They didn't necessarily make a counter to this. They just noted that the possibility was very slim.

I finally realized there was no getting around what needed to be done. Outside those few substitute suggestions I offered, I didn't try to fight the plan. I gave the approval for them to go forward. It wasn't as hard to accept as you'd think; I'd already gone through so much with having to make serious decision after serious decision. It was as if I'd become so accustomed to making them, they didn't even bother me as much. This one was just another added to the bunch. Tanndra just sat quietly during the entire conversation with the doctors. She had no questions for them or input. They could see she wasn't apprehending what was about to take place which ironically confirmed the very reason they wanted to move with this particular plan in the first place. At the end of the day the need for Tanndra to get better was dire. It could not be put on hold any longer.

I could not allow my personal wants of having more children get in the way of it. What helped give me solace was being thankful for the one child I was about to be introduced to. I anticipated my family of four living life as I envisioned and planned for us to. But as the old Yiddish proverb says, "Man plans, God laughs." Just because God laughs at our plans doesn't mean God abandons our plans. He only alters them. I'll take God's alteration over abandonment any day. If this was the plan God had for my life as a husband/father, I accepted it.

God had certainly done much laughing in my life the past few months. Seeing my wife for what was now a hundred straight nights in a hospital bed were not my plans. Not being able to experience the simple joys of the pregnancy journey were not my plans. Having to spend fifteen out of twenty-eight weeks of this pregnancy battling a rare brain disorder that destroyed our comfortable equilibrium were not my plans. To have expectations of a normal, healthy birth on February 27 be shattered by the bombshell of an involuntary, risky C-section on December 3 were not my plans. Sitting in a room surrounded by a team of doctors fresh off a final evaluation leading them to break the unwanted and unfortunate news to me that my first time having a child with my wife would be my last time having a child with my wife were not my plans.

After the doctors left, I waited in the hospital room reflecting on everything that transpired over the past couple of months. I couldn't help but think about one of the commonly said comments I'd received from most people through this anguish. "Wesley, I don't see how you're handling all of this so well. It's amazing." My casual response was, "I don't see how I'm handling it so well either." All night I thought about that mystery, determined (perhaps because nerves did not allow me to sleep) to figure out a true answer. What I'd realized after all that time was that despite countless moments of frustration, sadness, loneliness, disappointment, and stress, overall my soul and spirit has been resting in the bosom of a divine peace and tranquility so great that even though this situation was before me, it had not held me.

Had it poked me? Yes. Had it touched me? Yes. Had it prodded me? Yes. But it did not hold me. If it held me, depression would've caused my demise a long time ago. If it held me, lost hope would've left me with a languished heart a long time ago. If it held me, tears I cried would've led to a tipping point so overwhelming it may have been impossible to come back from. The reason it had not held me was because I'd been held by something else. God's grace. And God's grace is so robust that when held by it, there's no room available to be held by anything else.

Even though learning I wouldn't be able to have a house full of children as I wanted like Heathcliff Huxtable, Uncle Phil, or Carl Winslow to support, lecture and raise, I was resolute to be beyond thankful for the one gift God was about to give me in that of my son.

"Father…nevertheless, not my will, but yours, be done." Luke 22:42 ESV

17

My Prayer

"Hear my prayer, O God; give ear to the words of my
mouth."
— Psalm 54:2

December 3, 2015

The morning had come. We were scheduled to go
into the operating room at ten-thirty a.m. My mom
traveled back to Atlanta to be there. She had already
missed quite a few days of work the past few months
coming to check on us. Somehow, she made a way to
miss another to be there for the birth. She was steadfast
on seeing her first grandchild enter the world. Originally
the doctors gave one date to do the procedure, but had
to move it up a few days kind of at the last minute. For
that reason and because it was a Thursday, a lot of family
members were not able to be there but came that
weekend to visit. Tanndra's Aunt Frederica and Uncle
Chris who live in Conyers, right outside of Atlanta, were
present. They'd been a steady support for us over the
months sitting with Tanndra often times during the day
to give both me and Donya a break.

Uncle Chris was in the midst of a health crisis
himself fighting lung cancer. He had his surgery at
Emory Midtown as well and at one point during his
recovery was literally a floor above Tanndra. One night

Donya and I wheel chaired Tanndra up to his room where we had an exclusive mini family reunion. The laughs we had that night definitely gave us a temporary break from thinking about situations before us with two people we love dearly dealing with complicated illnesses. Despite Uncle Chris going through a painful threatening condition, he never worried about himself. He focused all his care and concern on Tanndra. Even after going home from surgery, he constantly came to check on Tanndra even if it was right after a long follow-up appointment on the other side of the hospital.

Tanndra's oldest sister Tammra hated she couldn't be there. She'd planned to come originally for the first date set, but when the change was made it conflicted with her schedule. Tammra was the sibling Tanndra had always been closest to. They're only eleven months apart. While all of her siblings share the same dad, Tammra and Tanndra are the only ones who share the same mom. After the death of their mother, they were committed to always having each other's back. There wasn't a day that went by they didn't talk on the phone or at least text. Therefore, it was very devastating on Tammra when Tanndra became ill. The person she trusted and could confide in the most was no longer accessible. On top of that, Tanndra was with Tammra when she gave birth to her first child Tyler two years earlier. Tammra had always hoped to be with Tanndra for hers but couldn't. Nevertheless, her love along with the love of all the rest of the family was felt and known.

I approached the morning as if I was getting ready to go into a competitive game. I suited up in my scrubs and was ready to go. My mind was focused on making sure Tanndra was as calm and comfortable as possible. Even though she still was moderately aware of what was going on, I could tell all the doctors surrounding us and walking the long hallway to the OR rattled her. While I viewed things as entering a game, Tanndra was literally about to enter battle. She'd never had surgery before. For this to be her first, it sure did hold a lot of complexity to it. Not only was she going to have a twenty-eight-week baby taken out of her, she was also going to have both of her ovaries removed as well. Even though I really had no choice but to make the decision for the doctors to take out her ovaries, I had the same feeling I had when I made the decision to keep the pregnancy. The fact that I was making a decision about Tanndra's body in which she could not cognitively decide for herself weighed heavy on me. I couldn't imagine being in her position. A very important part of her body was about to be confiscated never to be returned again, and she had no idea. I tried to put myself in her shoes. Excuse the wording, but all I could think about was my testes being removed without my knowing. The very thing that gave me the ability to have children gone all of a sudden and I wasn't even a part of the decision-making process. I hated it for her. I hated it for us. Though I'd come to accept it had to happen, my spirituality would not allow me to let go of the small centimeter of hopefulness that still existed about the matter.

I could not be in the operating room with Tanndra during the surgery prep. One of the nurses took me to a separate room to wait until they finished the prep and said she would come back to get me once they were ready to operate. The room was very small. I was too nervous to sit down so I remained standing looking at different medical FAQ posters on the wall. I didn't know how long the prep would take. After about ten minutes passed I figured it would be a while. I took a seat and began to think about the current moment.

There was still way more to what was about to take place than just the taking out of Tanndra's ovaries. While I believed the actual delivery would be successful, I could not say the same about the long term health of our son. Another huge factor spoken at the meeting we had with the medical team two days prior were the risks of delivering a baby so early. They relayed to us that at twenty-eight weeks we should not have any worries about the delivery. Studies showed at twenty-eight weeks there's only 4 percent chance of fatality in which doctors know the likelihood of it ahead of time from looking at ultrasound images. Our baby's images showed he was fine and healthy so there was no concern there.

My question to them was would he be perfectly normal and healthy. Their answer was babies born that premature live to be healthy 90 percent of the time, however it's depends on how one defines healthy. They were transparent by telling me there could be a chance of physical or mental defects. Sometimes babies born that early have special needs later on in life. Also with our baby specifically, the images did show that it could be a chance he had Septa Optic Dysplasia which could possibly affect his vision.

That was a lot for me to take in. I must admit while I accepted the news about the ovaries, I still had not accepted this particular news yet. I tried my best not to let it bother me the past two days. Now that I was forced into this idle quiet time alone in waiting, it crept up and began to burden me. The days leading up to the procedure I'd had so many family and friends say they were praying for us. As much as I loathe to confess, I had not taken the time to go into full blown prayer myself. The frantic and frenzy of preparing for this day consumed all phases of my life. I needed to pray, and I believe this time of waiting alone in this tiny room was divinely set aside for me to do just that as Tanndra was on the other side of the hallway receiving her epidural. I left her maternity floor room expecting to go straight into operation, but God had other plans for me to unexpectedly go into an unknown room for another type of operation. God needed me to operate my faith.

Sometimes God will redirect our travels into a place where we're forced to encounter him. That's why you shouldn't always get upset whenever the destination you thought you were headed hits a delay or dead-end. It could be God preventing you from reaching it at the time you expected because you won't fully receive the blessing your destination has to offer unless you reach it at the time God has appointed. It's your delay or dead-end that may provide you the only opportunity in which you have no choice but to talk to God. It's in your communing with God that you can recognize there are better outcomes within your destination you originally could not think of or foresee because you accepted being told there were no other options. However, God wants you to know that he is able to create options at any split second. And though God can do anything he wants to when he wants to, how he wants to, there are some things he waits for us to specifically petition him for before he decides to act.

As I sat in the chair I bowed my head and closed my eyes to speak my prayer:

"God. I know I haven't gotten the chance to really talk to you about all of this. My mind and emotions have been all over the place. It's as if I'm in a robotic trance just moving where I'm told to move. All the information given to me by doctors the past few days has submerged into a pool full of questions and doubts. I understand what must be done on their end. You already know our situation. That's why I'm coming to you right now at this last-minute moment asking for you to work a miracle. God if there's anything you can do to change the expectations of this procedure please do so. Please work a miracle in our lives right now, oh God. I know you have the power to do what the doctors can't do. I know you have the power to see what the doctors can't see. Lord please make a way for the doctors to find the source of this illness on just one ovary so that they don't have to remove both. My desire is to have more children with this one woman you have blessed me with. We've always dreamed of having a family with two or three children together. This sickness wants to kill that dream. God, rebuke it from doing any such thing right now in the name of Jesus. I call on you right now to allow Tanndra to walk out of that operating room with the ability to still have children. Although the doctors are saying one thing must happen, intervene on our behalf to make what they view as impossible happen. God I know you're able to do it. You're the only one who can do it. Work a miracle right now in the name of Jesus.

"Lord I pray that my baby boy I'm about to meet is in the cleanest bill of health. Tanndra is not the only one who's been going through. He has too. His connection with her being inside her womb has made him feel every pain, every discomfort, every injection, every infusion, and every relapse. Yet just like his mother he has fought like a champion. He has endured what most would have likely died from by now. God I credit that all to you. Since you've brought him this far already, Lord I pray that you allow him to be in full health. I pray there are no physical defects or mental limitations at birth or in the future. Let the delivery go perfect without any complications. Whatever the possibility of Septa Optic Dysplasia the doctors say he has, erase it right now God. Bless his eyesight and vision that he may have full use of it. I believe that you already have a special calling on this baby's life. I pray against any anomaly or abnormality that may try to get in the way of it. Lord, I pray he comes out into this world being favored and blessed. I know you're able to do it. Work a miracle right now in the name of Jesus.

"Lord, I pray for my wife. Cover her with your safety, protection, and grace as she gets ready to have this compound surgery. I know her mental stability has been damaged. I know her emotional stability has been tampered. But God, I pray that the faithful believing spirit she's always had is still in her. Give her peace in her spirit. Give her comfort in her spirit. Give her a serenity in her spirit to trust in you knowing you are with her all the way. God, she's gone through so much. Every time I think about it I want to cry. I don't know why this had to happen to her, but Lord I'm believing that you have something incredible for her after it's all said and done. This journey full of hurt, wounds, and turmoil will not be for no reason. I'm believing you have an awesome blessing in store for her that we cannot see right now. You've brought her too far to not have it in store. God, I pray her body goes through as little pain as possible. I pray she has a quick, comfortable recovery. Be with the doctors as they work on her from beginning to end. Allow her to walk out of this operating room not having the same condition she had walking in. Obliterate every trace of anti-NMDA receptor encephalitis. Put her on the path to getting back to herself being the lovely, sophisticated, motivated God-fearing woman you've made her to be. Watch over her, God. I place her in your hands right now. I know you're able to do it. Work a miracle right now in the name of Jesus.

"God, lastly I pray for myself. Give me the continued strength I need to be here for my family. They need my faith, prayers, and presence right now. Lord, I pray for a continued sane mind. It's been hard at times not to go crazy, but you've kept me leveled. Do not let me fall victim to stress, worry, depression, blame, or unbelief. I don't know how much pavement this road has left, but however long it is give me the durability and patience it takes to keep walking. Let me continue to be the best husband I can be. Let me hopefully be the best father I can be as I embark on this new phase of my life of fatherhood. I don't know exactly what it is you want me to learn from this experience just yet, but whatever it may be, I know it's going to make me a better man, better husband, better father, and better pastor. Keep me ground to stay the course, God. Give me power as I walk into this surgery to be Tanndra's support. As I'm standing to be her support, I ask that you stand to be mine. You've always been the head of our relationship and marriage. Despite the turns life has taken over the past few months, that has not changed for us. We still trust you and acknowledge you to be our Father and provider. Have your way in my life God. Have your way in Tanndra's life. Have your way in our son's life. Have your way in our family. I know you're able to do it. Work a miracle right now in the name Jesus I pray. Amen."

I felt a tap on my shoulder. The nurse said they were ready. I got up being prayed up. I left that room to go into the operating room. As I walked in I whispered one more thing to myself. "Lord, please hear my prayer." A major change in our lives was about to happen. The countdown was over.

18

The Miracle of Miles Wesley Thompson

"Out of difficulties grow miracles."
– Jean De La Bruyere

December 3, 2015

Walking into the room felt like I stepped into a freezer. The cold hit my skin as soon as I entered. The room was surrounded with white walls and white flooring. Tanndra lay on a table in the middle of the floor. I could see the upper half of her body; the lower half had a curtain like shield blocking my view. The doctors began working as soon as I took a seat next to her. Between the already befuddled state she was in due to the disorder and the lack of sensibility the anaesthesia now had her in, Tanndra looked and seemed as if she was flying high on cloud nine. I had to get close to her ear calling her name multiple times before she gave a very delayed response. Because I was sitting, I couldn't see the doings of the surgical procedure going on.

There were a lot of medical personnel in the room. I would say at least about fifteen doctors and nurses. Some were at the table doing their part in the surgery, while others were in the corner awaiting the baby. Those in the corner were from the NICU department. They had with them a large incubator to put the baby in as soon as the delivery was made. They gave me a rundown of what it would look like when they made the transfer from delivery to incubator. It would be a quick handover. They would let us see the baby for just a moment and then give him over to the NICU staff. They were then going to do their usual process with all babies who go straight to the NICU out of the womb. They warned me not to get scared or startled because it may look like something is wrong with baby from an outsider's perception due to all the shuffling, moving around, and insertion of tubes they do, but that's the regular course of action. They assured me the baby would be unhurt and in great hands.

My male ignorance led me to assume the C-section would take quite some time. I could not have been more wrong. To my surprise, all of a sudden the doctor said to get ready to pull out my phone if I wanted to record because they were taking him out. I had been in the room all of maybe ten minutes. I didn't think the delivery would happen so fast. I stood up as they lowered the curtain for Tanndra to see. She was still out of it and did not look up. Once I had full view, there I saw him. In Dr. Miller's hands was this long light complexioned beautiful baby boy. His head covered in smooth black hair. The sound of his voice through his cry introduced him to others for the first time. His comfortable setting in enclosed darkness the past six or seven months now being permanently interrupted as his eyes saw light for the first time.

I had prepared myself to see a baby the size of my hand. To my amazement, he looked much bigger than I expected. He came out at 2 lbs 8 oz and 15.5 in. The doctors and nurses raved about how cute and adorable he was. When asked if we had a name for him yet, I answered "Miles Wesley Thompson." Before she became sick, Tanndra and I had already chosen both a male name and a female name for the baby. Miles didn't have any significance to it. We literally just started randomly blurting out dozens of names one day sitting in our living room. When Tanndra said the name "Miles" we both kind of gave an expressive jump. "Ohhh, that's it!" I said. She had the same reaction saying she loved it also. So Miles it was. Of course, his middle name Wesley coming not only from me, but from my lineage. Wesley is the first name of my grandfather, father, and myself. I wanted to keep the name alive by giving it as his middle name.

My little man Miles was finally here. Fatherhood was official. Tanndra never looked at him. She had her eyes closed as the anaesthesia was winning the battle in the fight between it and her trying to stay awake. The moment was bittersweet because I did not get to share and enjoy it with her as I'd always imagined. Nevertheless, the general feeling I had was one of happiness and pride.

Just as they said they would do, the NICU team immediately took him over to the incubator to start their process. I had a little time to go over with them to take some pictures before Dr. Miller began the oophorectomy. I kept walking back and forth from the incubator to Tanndra trying to wake her enough to take a look at the baby. She did open her eyes to glance, but I don't think she was aware of what she was looking at. She was trying to talk but her speech was slurred. From the little I could make out, I could tell it was just gibberish.

Dr. Miller said the ovarian removal wouldn't take long at all. They pulled the curtain back up blocking the lower half of her body. I sat back down next to Tanndra holding her hands and whispering funny things in her ear to try to make her laugh. I told her the two of us produced a good-looking kid. She seemed to be a little more attentive and roused than she was during the delivery. She was able to shake her head signifying she heard and understood whatever I was saying. Hearing Miles still crying in the background, I squeezed her hand tight, put my forehead against her forehead, and told her I loved her. She told me she loved me back.

Even though I didn't get to have the moment I wanted with her during the delivery, I'll never forget this moment we had when she fought through the trance of all the medicine to tell me she loved me too. What made it so special was that for the first time in our eight-year relationship and almost three-year marriage, the words "I love you" came from an even deeper place in the heart. Loving her now was not just the same as loving her the day before. When I said "I love you," I meant I loved her not just as my wife, but now as the mother of my son I was just blessed to see with my own eyes. When she told me she loved me back it was not just as her husband, but now as the father of her son she just brought forth conquering so many odds doing so.

Despite all that we'd gone through and still faced, the world could not have felt any more perfect. Our situation may have spoken otherwise, but in that moment, I truly felt blessed. Little did I know I was about to find out that when you can feel blessed even though you feel you have nothing to show for it, God will do something wondrous in your life to make you blessed showing that faith is truly rewarded with favor.

Just a minute or two within the start of removing her ovaries, Dr. Miller said the words "I think we may have something here." She saw what she thought looked like a teratoma on Tanndra's right ovary. She called for the others with her to take a closer look and they all agreed. Dr. Miller stated it was very clear and visible from her immediate assessment that it was this right ovary which had what they'd been looking for all along. If so, they would only have to remove it and not the other. To confirm her supposition, they proceeded in removing just the right ovary and had it taken to the lab to test for a positive tumor or teratoma. The results would take about fifteen minutes. My heart was racing the entire time. I believe Dr. Miller's was as well. She was just as excited as I was at the possibility that a tumor of some sort was found.

After what felt like an eternity of waiting, someone in the lab called her phone with the results. It was positive! The right ovary had a teratoma attached to it. That was the source of the anti-NMDA receptor encephalitis. There was no need to take out the left ovary. Just to be sure, they compared it with the tumored ovary and it was no doubt that it was perfectly normal. All of that meant one important thing. We would still be able to have children. In fact, having kids would be no harder or easier than it would be if she had both ovaries. Dr. Miller educated me by letting me know that having one ovary gives a woman the same chances of becoming pregnant as having two.

The doctors concluded that the teratoma had been present on her ovary the entire time. It wasn't that it was too microscopic to see on the MRI scans, but it was likely the pregnancy blocked a clear view in the images for them to see one. It wasn't until they surgically opened Tanndra that they could plainly see with the naked eye the presence of a tumor/teratoma attached to one of her ovaries. Dr. Miller voiced to me how awe-inspiring it was to take in what'd just occurred. "All of this is truly a miracle," she said. The baby showed no signs of defects or ill-health. Tanndra only had to have one ovary removed leaving us with the opportunity to conceive again. Everything that was supposed to work against us before coming into this operating room ended up failing by time we got ready to walk out of the operating room.

I owe it all to God. The Bible says "The prayers of the righteous availeth much." It also says "Casting all your care upon God; for He cares for you." I've always wholeheartedly believed in the power of prayer. I can truly say what took place in that operation waiting room allowed me to experience the power of prayer. I've heard about, taught about, and preached about miracles. I can truly say with what took place in that operation room, I experienced a miracle. Everything I asked of God, God came through and performed. He knew my need, he heard my need, and he met my need.

I was left speechless and motionless. At the beginning of this story when Tanndra got sick I asked in a negative way the question, "Is this really happening?" I now found myself asking in a positive way the same question, "Is this really happening?" Did God really just show up for us like this? Did God really just do what the whole hospital thought was impossible? Did God really just directly respond to my prayer doing exactly everything I'd ask Him to do? Did God really just work a miracle in our lives before my very eyes?

The simple answer was yes. All of my fellow saints in the church who are reading this right now will understand the next statement following this sentence. I felt like shouting. After being told this procedure would end our ability to reproduce, God flipped the script and said this procedure would begin our ability to be living testaments and witnesses of his miraculous goodness. That's who our God is. God will take what was meant for bad and turn it around for our good. The things in your life others put a soon-to-be expiration date on, God will recondition with His inimitable extended grace and mercy.

I waved bye to Miles as they rolled him out to get set up in the NICU. The doctors wrapped up closing Tanndra and took her to a post-op room until the epidural wore off to where she could move her legs again. I briefly went back to her room on the maternity floor where my mom, Donya, Aunt Frederica, and Uncle Chris all waited to hear how everything went. I told them the good news and the joy on their faces was indescribable. They could not believe it. After months, everyone finally had a reason to smile and be happy.

The following days after the surgery would be crucial. According to the doctors, Tanndra would get significantly better since the teratoma was no longer inside of her. Speaking of the teratoma, I learned later that night there was another layer of madness that unfolded in our story. I knew that a teratoma was a form of tumor, but I didn't know exactly what kind of form until one of the doctors explained it to me in detail. In Tanndra's case she had an Ovarian Teratoma which was mature. According to cancerresearchuk.org, an Ovarian Teratoma is "a type of germ cell tumor. Germ cell tumors are cancers that begin in egg cells in women or sperm cells in men. The mature teratoma is the most common type of ovarian germ cell tumor. It is most often diagnosed in women during their reproductive years. It is often called a dermoid cyst. It is removed with surgery and the condition is then cured."[3]

---

[3] http://www.cancerresearchuk.org/about-cancer/cancers-in-general/cancer-questions/what-is-teratoma-of-the-ovary

To sum all of that up in relatable terms and as it pertained to Tanndra, the teratoma formed because of the pregnancy. Hence, the pregnancy is what caused the anti-NMDA receptor encephalitis brain disorder. The teratoma produced bad fluids that travelled up her spine reaching into the NMDA receptor of her brain.

It was because of Miles Wesley Thompson we got into this mess, but it was also because of Miles Wesley Thompson we now had this miracle as well. I could only hope the miracle was worth it all. For that to be, I needed to see Tanndra radically improve and be back home soon. Only time would tell in these next days.

19

Homeward Bound

"I long, as does every human being, to be at home
wherever I find myself."
— Maya Angelou

December 4 – 21, 2015

Just like with all C-sections, it took a few days for
Tanndra to get back walking on her feet comfortably.
Surprisingly, she was not in as much pain as the nurses
expected. They kept complementing how well and fast
her incision healed. Her quick healing was also present in
other areas. Just as the doctors said should happen,
Tanndra showed a sudden change in health after tumor
removal. There were no more inklings of hallucinations
or psychosis. She was able to communicate in a clear
logical manner. Her cognitive skills improved extremely
compared to the week before. It was even apparent that
she looked better. She had a glow and new look in her
face. It was as if her physical appearance felt the chains
break as a result of the surgery and couldn't wait to start
its approach toward a healthier look.

These were all good signs that hopefully we could be
on our way home again, but we had to take it one step at
a time. The first step was to move Tanndra from the
maternity floor back to the neurology floor. There was
no need to be in the hands of the maternity nurses any
more sense the baby was here. For the first time since

her hospitalization, the focus was now solely on her neurological issue. The pregnancy would no longer be a factor in the treatment process or how the doctors went about deciding things. The neurology team now had complete control of the situation without the assistance or tag team help of the maternal medicine team. Once the nurses saw she was able to get around okay from surgery and that the incision healed perfectly, Tanndra was transported back to the other side of the hospital to the neuro floor. All the nurses she had before were excited to have her back and had kept up with what'd went on. They too were overjoyed in hearing about the success of the C-section and miracle of the Ovarian Teratoma removal.

The neurology doctors informed me that their treatment plan was to do another plasmapheresis to remove bad plasma infested with negative antibodies still present from when the tumor was in her. Now that it was gone, the production of more negative antibodies wouldn't be possible. She would also have to receive Rituximab infusions every three months to kill negative antibodies likely still settled in her system. The doctors were hesitant to give me an exact date when she'd be able to go home. Christmas was almost three weeks away and as expected, my hope and wish was for her to be home by then. We'd already spent too many important days in the hospital. I definitely didn't want Christmas to be another one. The doctors said it was possible for her to be home by then, but also expressed to me not to bank on it. I was much more patient and understanding this time around than the last when I kind of edged in to get my way by having her discharged, only to realize it was a mistake. Once the plasmapheresis was completed, the plan would be to monitor her functions and ability and make a decision then if she could go home. The plasma exchange was set to take place the next week.

In the meantime, across the way, Miles was the new celebrity in the NICU. The nurses fell in love with him. My legs got quite the workout walking back and forth from Tanndra's room to the NICU. Going inside the NICU felt like entering the Whitehouse. There were a lot of security measures to pass by to get in. Although it was somewhat annoying, I did greatly appreciate it. It was good to know Miles was in a safe environment not accessible to just anybody. He had a spacey corner all to himself in the far back. The babies who needed the most attention were placed further back while the healthier babies were up front. The more Miles progressed over time, the closer they would move him to the front signifying he's closer going out the door to go home. Miles departure from the hospital would be based not so much on time passing by, but on him reaching different goals such as having his oxygen and feeding tube removed, sucking on a bottle, and being at a particular weight. I personally was in no rush for him to come home soon. My biggest anxiety was running into a possible situation where Tanndra had another serious relapse postponing her discharge and Miles was home before her. It would be pure madness trying to take care of a newborn at home while I still had a sick wife to care for in the hospital. I tried not to dwell on that thought much. I was pretty confident Tanndra would be in a position to come home by Christmas.

Miles body frame was so small laying in the massive cave-like incubator. At first I was too scared to pick up and hold him because I didn't want to do anything to hurt him, but the nurses forced me to get comfortable with it. I eventually got comfortable enough to grab him out of the incubator myself instead of having the nurses hand him to me. Every time I held him in my arm I couldn't help but think how much he looked just like Tanndra. He had more of her features than mine.

Tanndra's interaction with him was basically nonexistent at first. She honestly had no recollection of the C-section and was in a state of disbelief that a baby was now here. It saddened me to see the way she looked at him. It was as if she was observing some random child and not her own, which was no fault of hers. Her brain just couldn't absorb the reality that a baby which was just in her body was now laying in front of us to visually see and physically touch.

Thankfully after a few days her connection with him began to develop. She voluntarily asked to go see him instead of being pushed to. She held him for longer periods. She even started talking to him. The nurses wanted both me and Tanndra to spend as much time with him as we could, given the peculiar situation we were in being that Tanndra was still a patient herself in the hospital. They relayed to us the importance of "skin-to-skin" time for premature babies which Tanndra was willing to do.

Tanndra's connection with the baby wasn't the only one that developed more and more, but her connection with me did also. Our conversations started to feel like old times again. We laughed and cracked jokes together. We talked about possible plans for Christmas if she was out of the hospital in time. I felt like I was on my way to having my wife back again. When the plasmapheresis took place, she showed even more improvements. It was the first time she got the exchange while being completely conscious and she took it like a champ. I cringed again at the sight of the thick IV needle being inserted in the jugular vein in her neck, but she wasn't bothered by it.

Not long after, the biggest sign of improvement in my mind happened when one night she stood in the mirror fixing her hair and putting on makeup. Anybody who knows Tanndra will agree when I say she makes sure she's as presentable and well put together as anybody you'll find. She'd complained about the way she looked throughout her hospitalization, but wouldn't let anyone do anything to help her with it. Now she took the initiative to fix herself up. Seeing her meticulously beautify herself let me know that the real Tanndra was back. Maybe not completely, but just a little was enough for me to be pleased.

She was consistently in her right mind. Her blood pressure and heart rate were normal. She was eating well. She was able to physically get around without assistance. She was self-sufficient in various areas. This was the best shape Tanndra had been in since just days before we'd entered the hospital. The doctors were more than satisfied with her status, therefore they made the call to place a discharge date. It was set for December 21.

I was ecstatic as ever. My wife was coming home. This time by the order of the doctors instead of the order of myself. Tanndra had hoped to be home by Christmas just as much as I did. She grew so tired of being limited in the hospital room. She expressed how she felt she was good to go. December 21 was just a few days away when the doctors gave us the news. Like last time, I made preparations for her arrival by making sure the house was cleaned spotless. My mom and Donya had put up a Christmas tree and decorations one day without my knowing. I didn't mind because it did bring some spirit to the place. Tanndra and I had never decorated for Christmas since being married. I couldn't wait for her to walk in the house to see how nice and Christmassy it looked.

I asked Tanndra how she felt about taking a trip to Alabama to see family for the holidays like we were accustomed to doing every year. She declined saying she just wanted to rest and enjoy her own home. I was perfectly fine with that answer. We could've spent

Christmas in a dumpster for all I cared just as long as we were together and out of that hospital room.

In preparing to leave, I started packing up things that belonged to Tanndra in the room to take home. I didn't want to go through the hassle of doing it the day of discharge. It wasn't until I began packing that I realized just how much stuff we'd accumulated over time. Between her clothes, accessories, items I'd brought from home to help her remember things, and even my own clothes from staying so many nights, both my trunk and car were filled when I finished. It was perfect proof that this hospital had been a live-in home for us for four months. It was time to go!

December 21 felt like it took forever to come even though I just found out less than a week earlier she would be discharged. The hardest part about going home was leaving Miles behind. Even though we weren't with him 24/7, I still felt present and connected. I was told from family and friends that preemies usually went home around their original due date. If that was the case, we wouldn't have Miles home with us for another two months. While I hated that probability, at the same time it was somewhat of a blessing, because it gave us time to get adapted to life under new circumstances as Tanndra recovered. Though she was better, she was nowhere close to being well enough to care for a baby at home. Surely two months would be enough time for her to get to that point. Plus, nothing at home was baby ready. We had no crib. The guest room which was planned to be turned into his room was still the same. There were no bottles or toys. I didn't have the time to get all those things done dealing with so much. Perhaps it was a fun project me and Tanndra could get done together while we waited for Miles to get home.

The NICU nurses were glad to see us going home. They had been told of Tanndra's situation and really felt for us. They assured us Miles would be okay and to take care of ourselves as much as we needed. We would be able to call whoever Miles nurse was anytime day or night to check on him. We also had access to come in and see him anytime we wanted. Even if it was two o'clock in the morning. I'd planned to visit him every day. I couldn't see myself letting him go a day without seeing and touching his parents. He was slowly but surely growing. He remained in the incubator and still had a while before being taken out to be placed in an open crib. The NICU staff made it much easier for us to leave. They said most parents struggle going home leaving the baby to stay in the unit, but get used to it after so long. They even joked saying once Miles did come home, we were going to wish he was back in the hospital in their care. They definitely left me feeling better about the situation as we made our way back to Tanndra's room for one more last task before headed out the exit doors.

One of the nurses had to remove the IV from her neck used for the plasma exchange and bandage the insertion. The doctors wanted to leave it in just in case they felt there was a need for another exchange before discharge. If so, they wouldn't have to go through the process of sticking her again. Once that was done, I got instructions on what medicines to pick up from the pharmacy and what specialists to call to set up follow up appointments. I signed the discharge papers and that was it. We were set free. Unlike last time, Tanndra had a pep in her step and cheerful sensation about her as we walked out. It made me happy to see her happy about going home.

Donya was with us and was relieved that the day had finally come. She had plans to ride with Aunt Frederica, Uncle Chris, and their cousin Jonathonne to visit their family in Alabama for the holidays. She felt good knowing Tanndra wouldn't have to spend Christmas in the hospital. I looked forward to seeing her be able to get back to living her life now that we were out of the hospital. The way she stuck in the trenches with me the entire four months was truly amazing. No matter how much I tried to make her get back to living her own life, she refused to leave until Tanndra was in the clear. She knew I would have a heavy burden handling things by myself if she left. There aren't too many people willing to sacrifice the way she did on her own without being asked. I don't know how or when, but God is definitely going to bless her in a tremendous way for what she did for us.

The three of us walked into the December cold to the sounds of Christmas bells ringing and sight of Christmas reefs on top of poles lined down the street. It was a great day. It was sure to be a great holiday after all we'd endured. It was great to have my wife back. It was great to be homeward bound.

20

Not Again...

"The loneliest moment in someone's life is when they are watching their whole world fall apart, and all they can do is stare blankly."
– F. Scott Fitzgerald

December 21 – 22, 2015

Tanndra was more engaged this ride home than the last one. She didn't have the same dazed look on her face. She was talkative in our conversations with her. When we got home, she observed things in a way that said she truly missed the place. She looked comfortable walking around familiarizing herself with what had always been hers, but she'd been taken away from for four months. She noted how nice the Christmas tree and decorations were thanks to my mom and Donya. It was about eleven in the morning when we got there. Because of Tanndra's progression and previous setbacks, I decided to go into work later that day once we got Tanndra settled in. I knew she would be okay with Donya being home with her.

The benefit to working at a university is getting paid holiday breaks when the school is closed. Mercer was set to be closed from December 24 to January 4. It was perfect timing because it gave me two weeks to put all my time into being with and caring for Tanndra and

Miles. Donya had plans to leave on Christmas Eve to go to Alabama to visit family. She asked if I needed her to stay, but I happily pushed her to go. The last four months had been just as hard on her as they had been on me. She was long overdue for a break to get away. I told her I would be okay alone. In fact, it may have been better for Donya to leave for a few days so Tanndra could get back into the swing of things at home in a relaxed way. Not that Donya would cause distractions, but Tanndra had always been used to just the two of us being around. Donya totally agreed and went on to suggest that I try to do a couple of in-home romantic dinners and movies nights while she was away.

I was hyped about what I had to look forward to. Spending a nice romantic Christmas with my boo. Having her in my arms to hold tight and love on. Checking in on the progress of our son at the hospital with her at my side. Possibly going to church for Watch Night if I could get Tanndra to come. I couldn't wait to get the next few days over with to officially start my holiday break. The nightmare I'd endured for so long seemed to be coming to an end. Nothing could get in the way of ruining all the good things that were to come in the next two weeks. At least I thought it couldn't.

I started to get ready for work by ironing some clothes and taking a shower. Before getting in the shower I sat with Tanndra at the table to eat a snack. We talked a little bit before I got up to leave for our bedroom bathroom while she still ate. Donya was with her continuing conversation.

I was in the shower no more than five minutes when I heard a bang on the door. I thought it was Tanndra. She used to always knock on the door when I showered just to make me get out for no reason. I thought she was back to her old shenanigans, but then the banging got louder and more intense. Through the sound of the water hitting my head, I could almost make out someone calling my name. Thinking it was Tanndra I just replied with, "Yea?" I didn't hear anything except for more banging the door. I cut the shower off and heard my name called again. It was Donya frantically yelling, "Wesley, hurry up and get out here! It's Tanndra!"

I quickly jumped out of the shower, threw a towel around my waist, and swung open the door. What I saw was the last thing I could've ever imagined seeing at that time. Tanndra was lying on our bedroom floor having a seizure. Her body twitched from head to toe as she was in an uncontrollable spasm. I was immediately in a state of shock. So much so that I literally just stood in the doorway for a moment before making my way to her. Her head was stiffly turned to the side. Her eyes rolled to the back of her head. I yelled her name to try to get her to look at me but it didn't work. I noticed blood all over the carpet and some on my hand, but didn't know where it came from until I saw the bandage placed on her by the nurse dangling from her neck. Blood was spewing from where the IV needle was removed hours earlier. This freaked me out to the max. Initially I was fearful because I thought she was losing blood by the second, but then I discovered all the blood apparently came out at once and ceased. I figured the intensity of the seizure must've put pressure on what was still a fresh open incision which caused blood to eject the way it did. This seizure was just as bad as the others she had. Although this wasn't the first seizure we've encountered obviously, there was one big major difference. We weren't in the hospital. With the previous seizures, nurses and doctors were around to instantly spring into action. Donya and I had no idea what to do which made matters even more pressing and scary. Donya already had the phone in her hand calling 9-1-1 when I came out of the bathroom. She gave it to me to speak with the dispatcher who calmly talked me through some appropriate motions for the situation. She assured the EMTs were on the way and that things would be just fine if I stayed calm and made sure I did what she asked me to do concerning Tanndra.

I couldn't believe this was happening. Here I was in just a towel with water dripping down my body kneeling on my bedroom floor over a seizing, bloodied Tanndra. This was not where I expected to be after just getting home. Things had been almost normal; 20 minutes ago we were sitting at the table eating a snack together; she'd just been talking to me about our good looking Christmas tree. I'd been thinking about what movie to rent from Redbox for our upcoming date night at home. Ten minutes ago, I left a well-looking, well-recovering Tanndra. Now here she was possibly slipping into Lord knows what horrible condition before my eyes. Two simple words summed up what I thought about everything. "Not again…"

I looked up and noticed a trembling and crying Donya. This was traumatizing for her. She had never been present in the room when Tanndra had seizures in the hospital. This was Donya's first time seeing her have one, and it was while she was alone with her. I asked what happened. How did things turn so quickly?

She said not long after I left Tanndra complained about not feeling well. Donya asked if she needed to lay down and Tanndra said yes. Donya could tell Tanndra was kind of wobbling on the short walk from the living room to our bedroom. All of a sudden as soon as they got to our room, before she could make it to the bed Tanndra just fell to the ground and started seizing. It was so out of the blue. Just when I thought our journey thus far couldn't get any stranger, life answered with the rebuttal "Oh yea? Well let's see about that."

When the EMTs arrived they urgently got to work which allowed me to slip away to put some clothes on. They threw what felt like a million questions out at me. I explained to them she'd just come home from a long hospitalization and hadn't been home an hour yet before the seizure happened. In listening to their communication with one another while treating Tanndra, this was a very serious seizure. At one point, I overheard concern about her breathing. They loaded her up into the ambulance to be taken to Emory University Hospital St. Joseph's. I begged them to take her to Emory University Hospital Midtown where we'd just left so that the doctors and nurses who have been treating her could assess her. They made the claim that it was policy for them to transport to the nearest hospital, so Emory St. Joseph's it was. I told Donya to stay home and I would call her with an update as soon as we got there. She was still very shaken up and I didn't want to put her through any further disturbance. She needed to come down from what was a distraught emotional high for her.

I rode in the front of the ambulance. I didn't say much to the driver. I was too numb to say anything. Too numb to feel anything. I looked back through the window watching them continue to work on Tanndra hooking her up to different machines. I wanted to fall off the face of the earth. I'd finally reached my tipping point. I thought to myself, "How much more of this can one man take? How much pain and suffering can one man see his wife go through? How long can a man go through what I've been through before he just has no will or want to live anymore?" Honestly, dying didn't sound too bad of an option at that moment. I wasn't talking about Tanndra dying. I was talking about me dying. That's how numb I felt. The thought of death didn't bother me one bit because it actually sounded welcoming. Getting away from the chaos and rollercoaster of this situation. Handing over the management and responsibility of four months of craziness to someone else and just leaving for good.

I've often heard the scripture quoted, but for the first time I could categorically relate to David's words in Psalm 55 when he said, "Fear and trembling come upon me, and horror overwhelms me. And I say, O that I had wings like a dove! I would fly away and be at rest; truly, I would flee far away…" (Psalm 55:5-7).

I had to be real with myself. I was in a cathartic moment. It took this ambulance ride for me to crack the shell I'd wrapped myself in and admit to myself that life was jacked up. To admit to myself that I didn't want to deal with this anymore. I didn't want to handle more admission paperwork. I didn't want to talk to any more doctors. I didn't want to see another hospital room. It was all too much. I wasn't suicidal in terms of thinking about how I would actually end my own life, but I did think that dying was a better alternative than having to go through all of this again.

When we arrived at the entrance of the ER, I stayed in the ambulance while they unloaded her. I needed to collect myself. I didn't want to get out and go in until I was calm. I was in too sensitive and delicate of a mood to thrust myself back into a setting I thought was behind me. Just when I composed myself enough to be ready, the driver opened the door to tell me it was time to go in. They were able to settle down the seizing by time we made it to the hospital, but just after being placed in an ER room she transitioned into another ill-fated activity. She became erratic and hallucinogenic. It was a repeat of the first time this all happened in August, and the time we had to bring her back to the hospital after being discharged in late October. I didn't need to ask what was wrong with her. I already knew. She was relapsing. The question to ask was why.

The ER doctors had no idea what to do. I was able to rundown her four-month medical history to them verbatim which I could tell they were impressed by. As long as I'd been in the hospital conversing with doctors and nurses, I should've had an unofficial medical degree. I knew the exact terminology and vocabulary to use to describe her condition to them just like the doctors at Midtown would. I pleaded with them the importance that they get her transferred to the Emory Midtown location ASAP. Seeing that I clearly knew what I was talking about, they did not hesitate to make the call for the transfer. They'd spoke to one of the doctors at Midtown to get instruction on what to do while in wait for an ambulance to come.

The erratic body movement got worse. They tried to calm her with injections of Ativan, but just as before it didn't work. I put restraints on her to keep her from hurting herself. I called Donya to update her on the next move. She would drive to meet us at Midtown once we got ready to take off. I made phone calls and sent text messages to some close people. I had not told everyone about Tanndra's discharge. Only a few family and friends knew. They were devastated by her relapse. It hurt them that we were going through this yet again. It was as if life was toying with us for no reason.

When we got to Midtown it was quite late. I expected us to go back into the neuro-ICU, but instead they put her in a room on the general medical floor. Not the neuro general floor like she'd been on before leaving earlier that day. Whoever at Midtown received the transfer call from St. Joseph's seemingly did not digest in detail the severity of the situation. I expressed to the new nurse how imperative it was for Tanndra to be in the ICU, but in her view I didn't know what I was talking about. She leaned on what she thought needed to be done by the book and blatantly dismissed my suggestions. To say both Donya and I were ticked off would be an understatement. Only the on-call doctors were present. Luckily the doctor on-call was the family medicine doctor who'd seen Tanndra the day before. He was jolted by the sudden change that'd occurred in her. He recognized the need for her to be back in the neuro-ICU, but unfortunately there were no beds available. We had to stay put where we were until morning.

I was still wearing whatever I'd thrown on after taking my towel off when the paramedics came to the house. It had been about twelve hours since the fiasco. I demolished a McDonald's meal Donya brought me when she met us at Midtown. I hadn't eaten at all the entire day. I was ready to get the day over with, praying for better on the next. It took forever for Tanndra to get calm enough to go to sleep. I spent the night with her awaiting to see what the subsequent move would be.

The next morning one of the neurologists who'd seen Tanndra quite a bit came to see her and was mortified at how little care she'd received from the nurse overnight given the symptoms she displayed. Her heart rate and blood pressure levels were way too high when the neurologist checked it. The nurse hadn't hooked Tanndra up to a heart rate and blood pressure monitor to keep track of it throughout the night and early morning. The body movement had become more aggressive from the day before. It was glaring that she'd returned to a state of psychosis. To make matters worse, she noticed from looking closely at Tanndra's face and eyes that she'd been seizing. In fact, she was having a small seizure right then and there. I couldn't see it and neither could the nurse, but someone of the neurologist's expertise was able to notice it through the rigid movements of her twitching.

The neurologist was livid. Her fear was that Tanndra was possibly seizing all night in her sleep adding more damage to her brain from the previous seizures. She unleashed mayhem on the nurse. I must admit, I kind of savored in the verbal chastising she received. Perhaps she wouldn't have been reprimanded if she gave herself the chance to hear me out the night before instead of cutting me off assuming I had no idea what I was talking about. The neurologist called in a "code med" which signaled for a doctor from numerous areas to assist with the patient. They wanted to get Tanndra in the ICU as quickly as they could. The neuro-ICU was full, but a bed was expected to be available in two hours. They hurriedly transported her to the general ICU in the meantime to get her set up.

We were back in the neuro-ICU exactly two hours later. I have to give credit to the neurologist and neuro staff for moving so swiftly to make sure Tanndra was in the most suitable location fitting to her needs to receive the most appropriate care. It was odd walking in being greeted by all the nurses on a first name basis being that they'd seen my face every day for the past four months. I'd basically become a fellow co-worker. It was as if we were returning to our second home.

We were in a room on the other side of the ICU this time. I took a seat staring at Tanndra. We were at step one all over again. I was still in a disbelief. It didn't seem real. It didn't make sense. Just yesterday I was at home with this girl eating a snack. Now she was back in an ICU room with a feeding tube down her nose again. Just yesterday we were talking about Christmas plans. Now her ability to talk was eliminated because of a breathing tube down her throat. Just yesterday she was walking around our home admiring how much she missed it. Now she was lying motionless in a hospital bed intubated on a ventilator. This had become too familiar of a sight. I was tired of seeing my wife receiving assistance from a machine to breathe just as much as I'd seen her breathing on her own; I'd seen her lying down unconscious more than I had of her conscious.

It felt like someone snatched my heart right out of my chest. It felt like someone handed me an early Christmas present I really wanted, just to rip it out of my hands seconds later and walk away with it. Once more I thought to myself, "Not again." Not ICU again. Not a ventilator again. Not intubation again. Not more confusion again. Not more unanswered questions again. Not being in the unknown on how long she would be like this again. Not being worried about when we'll get to go home again. Not long nights spent in the hospital again. Not more meals in the hospital cafeteria again. Not more walking to and from the NICU again. Not being forced to question myself on whether Tanndra would make it through this time again. Not again. Not again. Not again.

"Not again" was an illusion. Reality was staring me right back in the face as I sat waiting on the doctors to come in with a report. It was December 22. Celebrating Christmas didn't look too promising.

21

Merry Christmas

"It's up to you to find beauty in the ugliest days."

December 23 – 25, 2015

The doctors were at a loss to what on earth caused the sudden relapse. They had taken every precaution in making sure she was well beyond a healthy enough state to go home the day before. Knowing she relapsed the last time we were discharged, they were intent in not letting her leave until they felt without a doubt her care could be managed at home. She'd gained remarkable progress after the removal of the ovarian tumor which was exactly what the doctors hoped for based off the case studies they reviewed. None of it made sense, but they were determined to get down to the bottom of it expeditiously. They knew how excited we were about going home the day before. As had been the case throughout our experience, they showed incredible empathy toward us. They promised me they were going to do all they could to get her back on her feet so that we could get back home as soon as possible.

No matter how quick they worked to fix things, I knew we wouldn't be able to go home within the next two days. I didn't give myself the chance to entertain the possible idea that we'd be home for Christmas. I'd accepted the fact that we were in for another long stay through the holiday. To take my mind off of the misfortune and calamity happening with Tanndra, I spent a lot of time with Miles to balance it with peace and smiles. He certainly brought a cheerfulness to my spirt I desperately needed. I looked forward to being informed on how much weight he'd gained every time I visited. Each ounce was an ounce closer to him being in complete nourished health. In a sense, I was jealous of him. There he was in his nice warm incubator oblivious to the trouble going on outside its four walls as his mother lay in an ICU herself. He was worry free. Life was new for him. He didn't have any strenuous responsibilities on his shoulders to take care of. He didn't have to juggle multiple tasks at one time or make serious life-affecting decisions. He was just chilling, being pampered 24/7. Holding him I said, "Son, I'd do anything to change positions with you right now. Your daddy struggling, little man." Of course I didn't expect a response, but it was good to talk to someone knowing the only thing they could do was listen. He didn't know it, but he hadn't been alive a month and already had a job as a therapist.

Donya questioned leaving the next day with Aunt Frederica and Uncle Chris to go to Alabama for a week or two. With Tanndra's sudden change, she felt she needed to change her plans and stay to help. I told her I would be mad at her if she didn't go. There was no need for the both of us spending Christmas in the hospital. I guaranteed her I would be just fine alone. Tanndra was my wife. Miles was my son. It was my duty and obligation to watch over them. Not anyone else's. She needed to take some time off to recover from the hectic forty-eight hours we'd just had. I told her to let her mind rest and not to even think about what was going on at the hospital. I would let her know if anything substantially changed.

The doctors fulfilled their promise in accelerated fashion in finding out what caused the relapse. They had an answer later in the day. They explained to me that somehow before being discharged Tanndra caught pneumonia. In fact, from the chest x-ray they did it was still in her. Tanndra had been on seizure medicine ever since September. She was still on it two days ago at discharge and was prescribed to take it every day at home. However, the dosage had recently been lowered since she hadn't exhibited any signs of seizure activity for almost three months. The doctors determined the pneumonia caused the seizure medicine to lose some of its effectiveness and strength. It was likely she had pneumonia for days meaning that the medicine had been nonexistent in working long enough for a seizure to occur. It would have happened if Tanndra was still in the hospital that day. The timing was just bad in that it happened soon after we got home.   I was glad to hear this was the cause instead of remnants of anti-NMDA returning being the cause. The plan was to give her some antibiotics to get the pneumonia out of her system. Once that was completed, they would start the process of weaning her off the medicine that kept her intubated so the ventilator could be removed. That would take at least a week though, which was something I already knew. It was possible for her to be discharged again by New Year's, but we wouldn't know for sure until she was completely awake off the ventilator and evaluated for a couple of days.

It was good news, but that didn't take away any of the despair I still felt. I was in such an unusual place in life. A place that thankfully not a lot of people will ever be able to relate to. My life seemed like something presented in a suspenseful movie drama. That evening I made a trip home to shower and grab a few things. It was late when I made it back to the hospital.

I walked through the entrance and was stopped by one of the security officers. Since it was after nine, I had to check-in at the security desk. I showed her my special care nursery parent badge so I wouldn't have to go through having them check my ID, type in my info, and write me a visitor's pass. As I flashed the badge she nodded with approval for me to continue to my destination, but only to stop me again. "The Neonatal ICU is this way, sir," she pleasantly said to re-direct my route.

"I'm here to see two people," I kindly responded. "My wife is in the Neuro ICU. I'm headed there first then on to the Neonatal ICU to see my son," I said while walking away in frustration. I wasn't frustrated with the officer. I knew she was only doing her job to keep the hospital safe. I was frustrated with the words that'd just left my mouth. It was in my response to her that raw reality hit me in the face. The security desk is in the center of the hospital. Making a left takes you to the Neonatal ICU, and making a right takes you to the Neuro ICU. I was standing in the midst of what divided the distance between my wife and my son. I was standing in the epicenter of two extremes. I was standing at the midpoint of what separated my family. I was standing in between a son whose condition was steadily improving in one ICU, and a wife whose condition just took an unexpected decline in another ICU. I was standing in between a rock and a hard place.

That phrase we often hear, "in between a rock and a hard place," has many definitions and interpretations. One being, "having only two very unpleasant choices." That definition soundly summed up how I felt. Making the decision of whom to see first as I walked through the entrance was one I usually didn't give thought to, but on this night before Christmas Eve it was one I struggled with. Although to the common mind it was a simple physical decision of pivoting my foot right or left, it was a tough emotional decision because when it came down to it I didn't want to be there in the first place. Why was I in a position to even have to choose?

I take pride in being a man and doing what a man has to do no matter what to take care of his family. However, at this moment I wasn't able to. Not because I didn't want to, but because I couldn't. And there was absolutely nothing I could do about it. I had no control over the situation. I'd seen my wife suffer for months in what had been physical pain, emotional despondency, and mental incapacity, and there was nothing I could do about it. I was only able to love on and care for my son in a limited manner and could sense he longed for the tenderness of his mother's touch but she was incapable of giving it to him, and there was nothing I could do about it. I had a family of three now. I was the provider and protector of the household. It was my job to keep everyone safe, secured, and sheltered, but they weren't at that moment, and there was nothing I could do about it. The only thing I could do was make the decision of whom to visit in the ICU first.

That was my life. The old Negro spiritual "Nobody Knows the Trouble I've Seen," explained it best. Nobody knew the trouble I saw, the trouble I felt, the trouble I suppressed, or the trouble I endured. I felt I was a living example what it was to be "stuck in between a rock and hard place." I was hopeful I wouldn't be stuck forever, but Lord knows I'd been stuck for too long. It was definitely not the Christmas Eve and Christmas Day I envisioned having, but as the darkness of the night eventually has to be overtaken by the sunlight of day, so does trouble have to be eventually overtaken by victory. The thing for me was that it felt like our victory was so far and remotely away.

Christmas Eve came the next day. I hadn't planned to do anything until two friends and former classmates Rich Havard and Kyle Stokes reached out to me to hang out. Both were in town for the holidays and doing some awesome things across the country. Rich was serving as the campus pastor for a ministry organization at the University of Illinois, Chicago. Kyle was in the first year of his PhD at a university in San Francisco. They talked me into getting away from the hospital for a few hours to take me to lunch and to catch a movie afterwards. It felt good to be out in a normal public atmosphere socializing with friends. I didn't realize how much I'd missed it. The rest of the day and night passed away quickly and before I knew it, it was December 25.

Christmas Day finally arrived, though it sure didn't feel like it being sixty degrees outside in Atlanta. Donya left for Alabama the day before. Both my family and Tanndra's family tried hard to talk me into coming at least for the day to get away from the hospital. They knew that sadly Tanndra was in a state of unresponsiveness. From their view, there was no point in spending Christmas in Atlanta by myself if she wasn't conscious. They thought it would do me well to come home to visit with family for just that day and go back to Atlanta the next day. It was tempting, but I just couldn't do it. I hadn't been home to see family the entire time Tanndra had been in the hospital, which was uncommon; I usually made a trip home at least once a month. I just knew I wouldn't be able to enjoy myself if I'd left. Conscious or not, I didn't like the idea of Tanndra being alone on Christmas. I'd already missed out on the joyous occasions of my birthday, her birthday, and Thanksgiving. I thought I had might as well make it a quadlet. I spent the entire day from the early start of morning in her ICU room.

I can't lie. It was one of the longest and most boring days I can recall ever having in my life. I spent much of the time fiddling around on my laptop. Matthew gave me a surprise visit. It was good to see and speak with him. We got in some good laughs as always.

Tanndra's best friend since third grade Heather and her husband Darrin were in town. Darrin had family in the Atlanta area they were visiting and planned to come by the hospital later. Heather and Darrin had come to see Tanndra early on in the hospitalization before she had the first seizure. They constantly called to check in through the months to see about her progress. Tanndra and Heather had a true close bond. It devastated Heather that Tanndra was going through this. I warned her in detail what to expect in looking at Tanndra when she came. This would be her first time seeing Tanndra on the ventilator and I didn't want her to break down at the sight of it.

I was not at the hospital when they came by to see Tanndra. My pastor's family invited me to their Christmas dinner that night. I declined at first because I was just in too down of a mood to go, but after eating what the hospital cafeteria called a "Holiday meal" my stomach told me to get out of my feelings and go eat a real holiday meal. The food blessed both my soul and my stomach. They had fried fish, turkey, chicken, mac and cheese, collard greens, and much more. My pastor and his wife Evelyn had visited Tanndra multiple times. They were so hurt to find out we landed right back in the hospital after going home. His encouragement to me from the beginning really helped me stay strong spiritually. He told me to just keep trusting God and believe that Tanndra was going to make it through. We had dinner at his daughter Pamela's house. She and her husband Jonathan were like a big sister and brother to me. My pastor's other daughter April and her husband Berwin were there also. They too were like a big sister and brother. April and I worked together with the youth ministry. From the moment I'd become a part of the church, their family had taken me in and treated me like I was their own. In fact, the entire church did. Out of all the churches I could have chosen to be a part of when I moved to Atlanta, I truly believe God led me to New Calvary Missionary Baptist Church. Living in a big city away from family can be tough, but New Calvary became a family away from family. I enjoyed the few hours I spent with them to eat, laugh, and pray. It was somewhat late into the night by time I left and made my way back to the hospital.

It was a rainy Christmas night. When I arrived back at the hospital, I sat in a chair next to her bed. I couldn't help but think about what Tanndra and I would be doing at that time had she never gotten sick. Ever since we dated we had a Christmas tradition. We would spend the early half of the day with my family, and the latter half of the day with her family. My family usually got together for Christmas breakfast at my one of my cousin's houses. Her Aunt Cathy always hosted an evening Christmas party we would attend. Often Tanndra got everyone to participate in games like Dirty Santa to end the night.

This Christmas was supposed to be a special one. When we found out we were pregnant, Tanndra and I talked about how exciting it was going to be knowing it would be our last Christmas with just the two of us. Tanndra with her love for fashion had even mentioned wearing a nice maternity Christmas sweater to rock the mature baby bump. We probably would've taken some Christmas pictures as a memento to look at years down the line reminiscing on our days without kids. With two months to go in the pregnancy, I'm sure we would've been drowned in gifts for the baby. It would have been perhaps the best Christmas we'd ever spent with one another.

Instead it was the exact opposite. This was no doubt the worst Christmas we'd ever spent with each other. But the blessing within it being the worst Christmas spent with each other, was the simple fact that we were still with each other. Even though one of us was conscious while the other was unconscious, we were still with each other. Even though one of us just ate a huge dinner while the other was on a feeding tube, we were still with each other. Even though one of us could talk to the other but the other could neither hear nor respond, we were still with each other. Even though on this rainy Christmas night we were in a room full of machines instead of a room full of family, we were still with each other.

That's why I refused to go out of town to Alabama for the day leaving Tanndra to be alone. There was nothing I could do to make the day a great Christmas, but it would still be a Merry Christmas in my eyes as long as I was with my boo. As long as I was with my bae. As long as I was with my wife. Because just a few days ago, I thought I was close to losing her again. There I was, a twenty-seven-year-old married man who'd for four months feared losing his wife to death not one time, not two times, but numerous times over the course of that time. I can't describe to you the overwhelming strain that caused my head and heart. But Tanndra was still here. Though she was receiving help breathing, at least she was still breathing. At least she still had a heartbeat. At least I could still touch her and feel warmth skin from blood running through her. At least I could stroke my hand across her face. At least I could still be with her as she laid in a hospital bed, as opposed to riding behind her in a funeral procession as she laid in a hearse.

If this experience had taught me anything it was to cherish life no matter how perfect or imperfect it is. A popular quote says, "Yesterday is history. Tomorrow is a mystery. Today is a gift. That's why it's called the present." Christmas day was my present because it was another day I was gifted to have Tanndra in my life after all we'd gone through. Despite her state of being, I didn't want to spend Christmas any other way or with any other person than with her in that neuro ICU room.

I turned the television and lights off and looked out of our third-floor window as the rain hit the ground. I grabbed some covers and prepared to call it a night. Before falling asleep, I bent down over Tanndra, adjusted the tube in her mouth to the side, and pressed my lips to hers giving her a kiss. I then placed my right cheek close against her left cheek and whispered in her ear four special words to end the day. "Good night. Merry Christmas."

22

Superwoman

"I'm a woman phenomenally. Phenomenal woman,
that's me."
– Maya Angelou

December 26 – 29, 2015

The next morning after the doctors made their morning rounds they gave me an update on where they were with Tanndra. The pneumonia was no longer present, thankfully. With the sole reason for the seizure and this particular hospitalization gone, they decided to the start the process of weaning her off the intubation medication in order to remove the ventilator. Knowing the length of time it took for her to be weaned previous times, the doctors were pleased to be able to predict that it wouldn't take long at all this time around. Their predication was correct. Two days later she was able to safely be completely off the meds and they took her off the ventilator.

When she woke up she was a little unsteady at first, but more aware than unaware. It did not take her as long to come to herself as it did last time. I assumed the fact she was only intubated for six days instead of six weeks made a huge difference. She recognized who I was and that we were in the hospital again. The ICU had become quite the familiar place for her to wake up to. She was totally competent in her thinking and speaking. She asked how Miles was doing, which was a great thing. It showed me that the small motherly instinct she'd developed was still present. It was obvious to me there were no effects of the brain disorder lingering to cause her to be confused or mentally muddled like I'd seen before. I explained what happened as to why we were in the ICU again. She had no recollection of anything that occurred immediately before the seizure. She remembered leaving the hospital, but that's it. She couldn't recall being home, sitting at the table with me, or talking to Donya right before the seizure took place.

I could tell by our conversation and the look on her face that she was troubled by not having any memory of it all. I could see her push her brain to the max trying to force herself to remember, but it didn't work. It bothered her even more to learn that Christmas had passed right on by. The one day out of the year everyone looks forward to was gone, and she had no idea of it ever coming. She asked me what I did for Christmas. I told her I spent it in the hospital by her side. She felt down about it. She didn't like that I had to spend it that way. Ironically, she told me I should've gone home to Alabama just like our family tried to get me to do. I relayed to her I was right where I needed and wanted to be, and that was with her.

The doctors were glad to see how well she was doing. She'd shown enormous headway and they were optimistic she would be able to go home in just a few days. There were steps that had to be taken for that to happen though. She couldn't be discharged to go home while in the ICU. She would have to be placed in another room on the general floor first. Because of another protocol, she had to stay put in the bed in her ICU room immediately coming off intubation. It was mandatory for her to have someone from physical therapy come to make sure she could move around and walk okay. I didn't like this rule because she wanted to go see Miles, but they wouldn't allow her out of bed to do so. When I visited him I took lots of pictures and videos to come back and show her. Once she started the physical therapy, I was able to wheelchair her to the NICU to see him. Although she was doing well walking around in the room and down the hallway, the nurses made her use a wheelchair to ere on the side of caution since the NICU was so far away.

Her visits with Miles were much better than they'd started off. I could tell she was building a sense of ownership of him. He was not just a baby, but he was her baby. There were a few visits where she'd stayed so long holding and looking at him that I had to hint to her I was ready to leave.

During her final physical therapy evaluation, I observed from a distance instead of being up close and helping like the other times. The therapist, Brittany, had also worked with Tanndra back in October when she was preparing to leave the ICU. As I looked at her blow the session out the water again—which put a huge smile on Brittany's face who'd grown fond of Tanndra—I couldn't help but be so proud of her. I thought about the resilience and grit she'd shown through so many ups and downs the past 4 months. It amazed me that she'd gone through the intubation process three different times over the last four months. To imagine the discomfort she felt after each extubation was impossible, but here she was days removed from unconsciousness on her feet and standing strong.

This short, five-foot woman had shown more toughness than any championship fighter. She was a fighter in her own right. She had gone through hell, but it did not take her out. She didn't look like what she'd been through by the grace of God. God's strength went to work covering her in the time of her weakness. Where others could've died, she lived. Where others could've been physically immobile, she walked. Where others could've given up, she kept pushing.

I knew I'd married an incredible and gifted woman, but it wasn't until now that I realized the courageous power she possessed. She was truly one of a kind. God knew this because it was he who made her. Therefore, he knew she held the perseverance and resolve within her to valiantly fight anti-NMDA. Even though the fight wasn't over yet, looking at Tanndra succeed in her therapy evaluation let me know that she'd at least won the first couple of rounds.

Tanndra and I had always viewed each other as equals in all aspects, but she'd now surpassed me. Instead of looking at her, I now looked up to her. She was my superwoman. She was my hero. She was my champion. She was my inspiration. I was mindful that this situation took a toll on me as a man, husband, father, and pastor, but what encouraged me to keep fighting in my own way was seeing Tanndra fight in hers. If she could come back and keep fighting after three intubations and three seizures, surely I could handle my fight. If she could come back and keep fighting after her C-section and ovarian surgeries, surely I could handle my fight. If she could come back and keep fighting after several chemo treatments, surely I could handle my fight. If she could come back and keep fighting after being a lower heart rate away from dying, surely I could handle my fight. Little did Tanndra know that it was by me watching her overcome her fight that she was actually helping me overcome mine at the same time.

After the session was over, the doctors transferred Tanndra to the general floor. Now all that needed to happen for her to go home was to maintain positive evaluations and observations from the doctors. They felt confident it would be by the end of the week. I honestly couldn't get excited at the thought anymore. We'd already struck out two times swinging at that ball. To protect myself from another disappointment, I chose not to buy in completely to the doctor's expectations. I just wanted to take it day by day and let things fall into place on their own. However, knowing I had a superwoman by my side gave me a buoyancy. Even if another setback did occur, there was no need to think the worst anymore. Superwoman had proved time after time again by this point that she may get knocked down, but she wasn't going to stay down. She'd proved that various barriers may come to temporarily stop the process, but they would never be successful in permanently stopping the person. She'd proved there was no limit to the number of comebacks she had left in her every time something went abhorrent. Just like a superwoman should, Tanndra proved these things not with words but with action. She'd already showed everyone on her medical team just how mighty she was. It would be great if we got home the next few days and actually stayed without another mishap arising, but if we couldn't then so be it. It would just be another phenomenal scene added to the continuing astonishing story of Tanndra, my superwoman.

Her many battles had wounded her. The scars and bruises marked her soul. She had long forgotten how to smile, how to laugh. But she was not weak and she was not afraid. She was brave and she was a warrior. Who stood toe to toe with death, with pain, with loss, with life. And she fought ferociously with her soul covered in war paint. Hiding her scars, her bruises, her weaknesses. And though she had lost many battles, she would win the war.

- the Morr.I.Ssey

23

Leaving it All Behind

"There is meaning in every journey that is unknown to the traveler."
– Dietrich Bonhoeffer

December 29 – 31, 2015

The date was set. Tanndra was ordered to be discharged December 31. Exactly ten days after the abrupt seizure brought us back to the hospital again. The doctors did multiple evaluations over the three days she was on the general floor after leaving the ICU. They wanted to make sure she was clear and ready to go without concern. They even did a test on the day of discharge just to make sure there wasn't another surprise presence of pneumonia. The speed of her turnaround was amazing. We were headed home on New Year's Eve when just a week earlier she was hooked up to a breathing machine on Christmas Eve. I had no preference for her to be home by New Year's like I had for her to be by Christmas when we were last discharged. I made it known to the doctors that I was in no rush this time around. I wanted her to be discharged whenever they felt we could go home without any possibility or chance of having to come right back like we had twice before. They agreed with me and though this current discharge felt rushed, they told me that they were beyond confident she would be okay. They had no timetable for her to be home by a certain date themselves. It just so happened that it fell on New Year's Eve.

Though Tanndra was doing exceedingly well according to what the doctors were looking for in evaluating her, there was another issue not physically related that began to sail into the shore of her being and anchor her down. I could sense depression was creeping in on her. As she now regained some limited control of her thinking and other cerebral abilities, she was finally starting to understand the scope of things that'd happened. Not necessarily understanding the intricate medical reasoning and components that got her to this point, but understanding the obvious yet tough reality that life was not the same anymore. She was reminded of it every time she glanced at the mirror near the hospital bed.

Multiple IV pokes on her arms and neck had left a lot of scars. The healed wound from the tracheostomy left an impressive blemish on her throat. Coming into the hospital in August she was 145 pounds, and now leaving the hospital she was 105 pounds. Being on a feeding tube pretty much the entire time left her with devastating weight loss. When she looked in the mirror, who she saw was not the beautiful healthy person she was accustomed to seeing all the time. In her eyes, this was a total stranger. Something came and totally transformed her body.

It wasn't just her altered physical looks that made her unhappy. It was also not being able to understand in detail her medical condition. I'd repeatedly gone down the litany of things that transpired from the very beginning explaining to her what happened, but she couldn't follow it. She wanted to know what happened, how it happened, and why it happened, but was not cognitively able to grasp it all which was crushingly frustrating for her. She sat up in the bed shaking her head telling both me and herself, "I just don't understand any of this." I tried my best to encourage her by telling her not to focus on it and that it would eventually all make sense to her. I wanted her to focus on how she did a good job making a quick turnaround in her health and to maintain it once we got home. Nevertheless, I felt for her. I'd always disliked seeing Tanndra sad about anything. I would do anything I could in my power to make her happy through a brief smile or a random laugh. I honestly did not know what to do this time. She had every right and reason to be sad.

Yes, it was a good thing we were about to go home, but we weren't going home to what we'd always known home to be. We were going home to something completely different. We were going home to a different life. We were going home as two different people now. Going through this traumatic experience had made us different in our own ways. Just from Tanndra's perspective alone, she was about to go home without a job or the ability to work for the next two to three years according to doctors. She was about to go home not being able to drive for a couple of months. She was about to go home no longer having the responsible independence she'd worked so hard to build for herself since she was fourteen when her mother died. She was about to go home prescribed to take twenty-six pills every day. She was about to go home without getting to take the baby that she couldn't even remember giving birth to, with her.

I was about to go home not knowing if I could manage keeping my job or not. I was about to go home to spending days of making phone calls to insurance providers, ambulance billing services, hospital billing services, and an abundance of other important services I'd put on the backburner to make sure we had things in order. I was about to go home being responsible to make sure Tanndra took all her pills every day. I was about to go home to welcoming in home healthcare nurses every week to check in on her. I was about to go home being responsible to make sure she got to and from what seemed to be twenty follow-up doctor appointments with different specialists over the next few weeks. I was about to go home doing my best to still try to find time to go to the hospital to visit Miles while also taking care of Tanndra. I was about to go home being not just a husband, but a medical caretaker.

It had set in for Tanndra that anti-NMDA receptor encephalitis had and was about to forever change our lives, but I refused to let it ruin the special day before us of going home. I knew more challenges were ahead for Tanndra physically and emotionally, but what gave me hope that we would get through them just like we'd gotten through the challenges of the last several months was the significance of our discharge day. The day was here. December 31. With doctors pleased, nurses happy, and bags packed, we were headed on our way out of the hospital again.

In what would be our last and final discharge from the hospital, I don't believe irony played a role in it being on New Year's Eve. I believe spiritual factors were in play. It wasn't the doctors who randomly chose this day for us to leave. This day was specifically appointed by God for us to leave. There was a deep divine significance in us leaving on the last day of the year.

We'd spent the last half of the year battling in the hospital. We'd spent the last half of the year battling anti-NMDA receptor encephalitis and everything that comes with it. We'd spent the last half of the year battling rapid heart rates, high blood pressure, psychosis, hallucinations, seizures, ventilators, intubated comas, chemotherapy, plasma transfusions, rehab, and relapses. We'd spent the last half of the year battling making life or death decisions for both Tanndra and Miles. We'd spent the last half of the year battling making medical decisions like ovarian surgery that would have irreversible lifelong effects. We'd spent the last half of the year battling not knowing if we'd have a healthy baby, or a baby at all for that matter. We'd spent the last half of the year battling not knowing if Tanndra would survive after another seizure or relapse. We'd spent the last half of the year battling the nearness of death almost happening in the blink of an eye.

Leaving the hospital for the last time after all these battles was God's doing. It was God's way of saying, "I'm not going to allow the battles you've fought this year be taken with you into the next year. The place you've spent half a year in will not be the same place you start this next year in. Everything you've been through in 2015 is going to stay in 2015. I'm not going to let it follow you into 2016; 2016 will be a new start. It won't be an easy start, it won't be a comfortable start, it won't be a stress-free start, but it will be a new start to a new life. This hospital is a representative reflection of everything you two have been through. When you leave this hospital for the last time, you're also going to leave behind everything 2015 took you through. All the battles will be left behind. All the fear will be left behind. All the decline to physical health will be left behind. All the encounters with death will be left behind. I'm leaving it all behind for you!"

As Tanndra and I walked out the exit door of the hospital, we were walking out of everything the hospital had represented for us. We weren't just walking out of a door, we were walking out of a year. We were walking out of a year of battles. We were walking out of a year of pain and suffering. Stepping foot out of the door into the chilly breeze of the air, we were stepping into a new year. We were stepping into a new start. We were stepping into what I hoped would be a year of recovery, restoration, and overflow: recovery of Tanndra's body being holistically healed in completeness; restoration of Tanndra's health, her mental stability, and emotional strength; Restoration of everything anti-NMDA had taken away from us; and lastly, overflow of God's blessings in our lives for staying faithful and true to him during this ordeal. In those four months, I questioned God. I got upset with God. As the disciples did during the great windstorm that came upon them in Mark chapter 4, I wondered if God even cared about us. However, I never stopped trusting in God. I never stopped believing in him. Even though my faith was challenged, it never ceased. God rewards those who are faithful to him, and my prayer was that my faithfulness to him would manifest in overflowing blessings for our family.

Tanndra and I had missed so many special moments together, but now on the last special occasion of the year, we would actually get to share it together unbound from the hospital. Traditionally Tanndra and I attended church for Watch Night service every year on New Year's Eve night to bring in the New Year. Watch Night is a religious service held the last night of the year where people gather in church for a worship service to renew their covenant with God, give thanks to God for bringing them through another year, and praying for blessings into the New Year. Specifically, in the context of the African American church, Watch Night service originated on December 31, 1862 when the slaves came together in their churches to await news and confirmation of the signing of the Emancipation Proclamation by President Abraham Lincoln. The executive order went into effect at midnight on January 1, 1863. All slaves across the country were legally declared free. It is said that when the news was received while gathered in the church, "there were prayers, shouts and songs of joy as many people (slaves) fell to their knees and thanked God."[4]

Being fresh out of the hospital, I of course did not take Tanndra to our church New Calvary Baptist to attend Watch Night service like we'd done every year of our marriage. We stayed home for her to get continued much needed rest. However, the spirit of Watch Night was heavily felt by us that New Year's Eve. God had signed our own personal specialized Emancipation Proclamation papers freeing us from a four-month enslavement to the hospital due to anti-NMDA receptor encephalitis. It went into effect as soon as we walked out of those hospital doors. I didn't need a church to pray. I didn't need a church to shout or sing songs of joy. I didn't need a church to thank God. I did all of that right where I was. Despite all of the hell we'd been through, I could still look back over the past year and say "Thank you, God!" Especially since freedom had come on that last day. We hadn't had much to celebrate that year, but nothing could take away my celebration of walking out the hospital the last day of the year with Tanndra by my side. There were so many times I almost had to walk out of that hospital alone without Tanndra ever coming out with me, but God saved her life. God preserved her life. And something tells me that down the line when this story is completed, God is going to use her life for his glory. God is going to use our story for his glory. In fact, even though our story has yet to be completed after nearly eighteen months of its beginning, it is my prayer that God is already using it for his glory, starting with this book.

Looking back on it, I truly believe leaving the hospital was symbolic of leaving behind all the hurt that

---

[4] http://www.aaregistry.org/historic_events/view/first-watch-night-service-occurs

consumed our lives. Leaving it behind didn't mean the aftermath effects from the hurt wouldn't still be felt. Scars and wounds, both literal and figurative, would no doubt continue to exist. The only thing left to do from that point was hope and pray for better ahead. Understanding that getting to better involved going through a process. A process that we're still in even as I'm writing these words now.

I didn't know at the time, but the four months being in the hospital was nothing compared to the months of recovery ahead of us. Those who've gone through extensive hospital stays that caused life changes can agree when I say that the real hard work isn't being in the hospital, but it's getting home from the hospital trying to adjust to new life while recovering. What you've read to this point is just a third of our story thus far.

New Year's Eve we left the hospital for the last time in regards to not staying overnight, but the very same hospital would go on to be a place we walked into daily for months while the third and newest member of our family had a few more battles to get through himself there.

I look forward to hopefully telling you about it by picking up from here to continue our story. If this book accomplishes the goals I've prayed for, I'm sure you'll be able to read part two in the future. The goals I had for this book are simple. I wanted to tell an unfortunate and tragic yet extraordinary and powerful story about a young married couple deeply in love whom while in the midst of things going great in life, were chosen by God to be used. God chose to use us as His servants to show the world that in the rarest of situations, He is able to do the rarest of things in that of performing miracles. My goals were to speak on how I went through and handled our experience from four different perspectives: as a young husband, as a man, as a father, and finally as a pastor.

To the couples who've read this, love each other unconditionally. Mean what you say when you repeat the words, "In sickness and in health," at the altar and stay true to them no matter what obstacles come your way or how early they come. Stay true to them not because you feel obligated to. Stay true to them because you want to. When tough times come you will know where you stand in your love for him/her by the reason you give yourself when you ask "Why am I still here?" The answer shouldn't be, "Because I have to be here." The answer should be, "Because I want to be here." Obligation has the possibility to fade. Want and desire does not. That's real genuine love.

To the men who've read this, don't be afraid to demonstrate your feelings in your most vulnerable moments. You can't always be thick-skinned. There will come times when your heart is unguarded because an event so crushing took place in your life. Allow yourself the room to express appropriate emotions and know that's what truly being a man is about. You hurt yourself and others around you when you try to protect from coming in that which has already been accessed. It's okay to be hurt. It's okay to show hurt. It's okay to talk about hurt. Those are the only ways you'll be able to get yourself through the hurt.

To the fathers or soon-to-be-fathers who've read this, know that your children (child) are truly gifts from God. They deserve your love and care. Try not to always place a gender role in how you take care of them. You'll never know when you may find yourself in the position to be both father and mother if anything unfortunate happens. Enjoy every simple moment from conception, to birth, to actually raising your child with your significant other. Not everyone is fortunate enough to have the opportunities to take in those simple joys. Embrace them as they come.

To my fellow ministry colleagues who've read this, take the challenge head-on when you find yourself in situations where you must live out what you speak out. When the cross you wear transforms into being the cross you bear, know that you're not bearing it alone. We all know that ministry can be a lonely isolated place. Not everyone understands us, even some of those who call themselves fellow laborers of the Gospel. Make sure you surround yourself with the right people in your broken moments. God won't put more on you than you can bear, but it can sometimes be just enough to make you feel the bearing is about to fall into pieces any second. Hold on and don't quit. I'm not telling you anything you don't already know when I say God will never leave you or forsake you.

Speaking of leaving it all behind, I pray that with this book I leave behind blessings and hope to all of you. If there's just one thing, big or small, you can take away from this book that positively impacts your life my job is done. I'm satisfied. God has used me and used our story to influence others in an uplifting manner. Our story is still being written. There's much more to still be discovered. The vow "In sickness and in health" is still active. I ask for your prayers as we continue our journey. In the meantime, whatever your struggle may be right now, know that it's not unbearable. God built you for it and it for you. God is using you for a purpose. You too have a story that God seeks to be glorified through. To God be the glory.

24

To God Be the Glory

"The greater the obstacle, the more glory
in overcoming it."
– Molière

April 24, 2015

Rewind eight months. Four months before the journey you just read about ever came into fruition with Tanndra becoming sick in August. It's April 2015. While I've just given the formal conclusion to the main part of our story in the previous chapter, I want to end this book on a note that is sure to show the power of God even more than has already been shown in reading our story. This is something that took place long before Tanndra became sick, but is still connected to our story. It is something only a handful of people know. It is something that many in our own family are about to find out for the first time while reading this. I've been very open in sharing our situation through this book. I would be remiss if I didn't include this one amazing happening that truly highlights the fact that God is real and is still doing miraculous wonders 2,000 years after the resurrection of our Lord Savior Jesus Christ.

Miles was not Tanndra and I's first pregnancy. We were actually pregnant for the first time in April 2015. Tanndra feeling a difference in her body took a pregnancy test one Sunday evening and it was positive.

We weren't trying to get pregnant so it came as a huge surprise to us. Nonetheless we were elated from the news. Both of us had smiles the rest of the night as we stayed up talking about what the next couple of months would look like. A few days went by of continued excitement as we tried our best to keep the news to ourselves. We wanted to tell family so bad, but wanted to wait to come up with a creative way to do so. Until then it was our little secret. That Wednesday Tanndra complained about stomach pains, but didn't think too much of it to be overly concerned about it. The next day and night the pain worsened. It was a pain she'd never felt before. That's when both of us became scared.

We went to the ER early that Friday morning to figure out what was wrong. While in the ER room explaining to the nurse what was going on and that we recently found out we were pregnant, they took Tanndra into another room to do a test of some sort. I couldn't go back with her. When they came back, I could tell the news wasn't good from the look on Tanndra's face. She had a miscarriage. It was just something that randomly happened. The doctor explained that miscarriages early on in first time pregnancies are more common than people may assume. Of course that didn't help the pain we felt, especially Tanndra.

It was unbelievable. One's week couldn't be so different from beginning to end. We literally started off the week on the highest of highs finding out we were pregnant that Sunday, just to end the week five days later on the lowest of lows sitting in the ER learning of a miscarriage that Friday. Tanndra took a much bigger emotional hit from it than I did. It took a few weeks for me to see her back to herself again emotionally. 2015 wasn't just a bad year for us because of the latter half as this book has expressed. We had to deal with a miscarriage as well months prior. As you can imagine, Tanndra went through a lot in this one year.

When we found out we were pregnant with Miles in late June it came as a surprise as I mentioned back in the beginning of the book. We weren't trying to hurry up and get pregnant again after the loss of our first pregnancy. Like the first time, the second pregnancy just happened out of nowhere.

Now you may be asking the question what is the point of me relaying all of this history and information. I did so to set you up for one heck of a powerful miracle.

That week of the first pregnancy in April, Tanndra used a pregnancy app to calculate the due date of the baby. We never did get to go to an official OB/GYN appointment so the app was all we had to go by. The app had her being due in the first week of December.

When we became pregnant with Miles and were able to go to a few appointments before Tanndra got sick, the doctor put his due date for February 27. As you've read, because of the brain disorder and need for Tanndra to undergo aggressive treatment the doctors had to bring Miles early. He was not supposed to be here until February, but our situation brought him early in the first week of December.

The baby from the first pregnancy was due to be here the first week of December, but that pregnancy was taken from us. Another pregnancy was later given to us and because of extenuating circumstances, that baby just so happen to come into our lives at the exact time the first baby was set to come into our lives.

The preacher in me is hoping none of you just missed your shout right there. I can't help but believe that was all God. Only people who can read what I just wrote through spiritual lenses can really grasp the supreme presence and power all over it. Let me try to make it plain.

That which God took from us in April that was set to come to us in December, God gave back to us in June. When he gave it back to us, he then divinely manipulated chronology turning what was supposed to be a forty-week pregnancy into a twenty-eight-week pregnancy. For what reason, you ask? So we could get what he gave back to us at the original time He intended for us to have it in the first place. In other words, anti-NMDA receptor encephalitis didn't have a grip on us. God had a grip on anti-NMDA receptor encephalitis.

That's a word for somebody reading this right now. You've lost some stuff in your life you were really looking forward to seeing grow. Some stuff got taken away early from you that didn't develop into what you know it could have been. God is wanting you to know that he is able to give you back what in some cases he took away, and when he gives it back, the fact that He took it away to begin with is going to make it even more special. When God has something for you, you will have it no matter what obstacles may get in the way trying to impede on it.

God said in April we were going to have a baby in December. Even though we lost that baby, behind closed doors God was doing his divine work saying to himself "they're still going to have a baby in December." Because when God speaks something into existence, it has no choice but to happen. That's why Isaiah 55:11 says, "So is my word that goes out from my mouth: It shall not return to me empty, but will accomplish what I desire and achieve the purpose for which I sent it."

My brother or sister don't dwell on what you've lost. Know if God truly meant for you to have it, he's going to give it back to you. Like us, you may have to go through some trials, troubles, and tribulations to get it back. But that makes for an even more powerful testimony in the end when you have a story to tell about

God's restoration in your life. I thank God that He saw fit to restore by giving us a true miracle baby in that of our son Miles. When I think about it I can't help but say to myself lyrics written by the late great Andre Crouch:

To God be the glory. For the things He has done.

About the Author

Wesley Thompson is a native of Florence, Alabama. He is an ordained Baptist minister and has served as a youth pastor and interim pastor in his eleven years of ministry. He graduated with a bachelor's degree in political science from the University of North Alabama and with a master's of divinity degree from Mercer University. He is currently pursuing a doctor of ministry degree from the Interdenominational Theological Center. He has worked as a college admissions recruiter and adjunct professor. He is a member of Alpha Phi Alpha Fraternity, Inc., NAACP, the Academy of Preachers, and various community service organizations. He is married to Le'Tanndra Thompson and they have one son, Miles Thompson.

9 780997 679786